INTRODUCTION

I started this book fo~~r my nephew Otello and~~ niece Ruby...they were approaching adulthood and I wanted to share some life learnings with them.

Little did I know I'd soon be sharing it with actual "adults" and the world!

In studying what was unique about what I had to share, two important themes arose:

1) Enlightenment – The attainment of spiritual knowledge or *insight*.
2) Entrepreneurship – The act of being an owner or manager of an enterprise who *creates* value through risk and initiative.

Enlightenment and entrepreneurship go hand in hand – the greatest *insight* I had in writing this book is that the most important thing in life is to *create*.

I believe that everyone has a book (or a poem, a sketch, song, etc.) in them. And not only do we have an *opportunity* to create, we have an *obligation*.

Creation is what leads to the vitals in our life: shelter, food, friendships, jobs, etc. And *you* wouldn't be here if it weren't for an act of *creation* by your parents.

Most of my creative energy has been applied to business...that's the key lens in my life. In business, the ultimate creativity is creating a new product or business.

But most of the rules of entrepreneurship apply to creating in life too!

Back to Miles & Ruby...

I traveled to see them carrying an early edition of the book of 40 of my life-learnings packed in my bags.

When they caught wind of that, they snuck into my backpack, grabbed the book and began to read...and they didn't put it down for 30 minutes!

I was so pleased with their engagement that I snapped this pic!:

I eventually took the 40 learnings, expanded it to 57 and that is the book you are holding right now.

My hope is that sharing my 57 learnings will support my life purpose: "to positively vibrate the Universe through my friends, family, colleagues and even strangers. "

Enjoy!

Table of Contents

Heart

Passion and Purpose

Getting Results

Body And Mind

When It Gets Stressful

Business Basics

Communication

Leadership

Hiring And Firing

Heart

3 Things Old People Wish They Had Done More Of

Last year I attended an amazing workshop called Coach for America led by former NFL player (and now coach and Minister) Joe Ehrmann — Joe mentioned something that truly changed the way I think about my life.

He referred to a study of older people who were in the "twilight" of their lives; and the study asked these wise elders a powerful question: What do you wish you had done more of in life?

Their answers were profound. Here they are:

1) Left More of A Legacy

What do we mean by legacy? I like this definition from Dictionary.com :

"Anything handed down from the past, as from an ancestor or predecessor"

This really resonates with me. As I get older, and read more about smart folks who've lived longer than me (Benjamin Franklin, Warren Buffet, Charlie Munger), the subject makes more and more sense. A legacy is your gift to those who will follow you — does it get any more important than that!?

Examples of legacy:

- In business, your legacy could be a company or product you build.

- In the arts, legacy could be a book, music or paintings you create.

- In family, legacy could be your children, grandchildren, nephews and nieces.

This book is an example of legacy for me – is there a legacy you've been meaning to create lately!?

2) Reflected More

When I heard old people wished they had reflected more, I have to admit I scratched my head. After all, if they're in their twilight years don't they finally NOW have plenty of time to kick back in their rocker and reflect?

But then I sat with it for a bit...and it made sense. Old folks wished they had more often gone to the proverbial "top of the mountain"...to think! In business, I call this "zooming out."

I believe THE #1 challenge that most people have is taking the time to zoom out, get altitude. A mentor of mine Ralph calls this time "sitting under the apple tree."

In fact, if you read my How To Innovate: The Five Things Top Innovators Do, you'll remember that the most effective thing you can do to innovate is to "Connect" or "Associate" things that you're observing in life. That's certainly a lot easier to do if you're "sitting under the apple tree." One way innovators reflect more is to travel outside their country — that really allows you to reflect on your life.

3) Taken More Risks

Old folks also wished they had taken more risks in life. This old adage comes to mind:

"You don't regret what you do, only what you didn't do."

I'm not just talking about physical risks/extreme sports type stuff — like when I jumped out an airplane in New

Zealand or hang glided in Rio, Brazil (neither of which I'll choose to do again!). I'm talking about taking more risks in day-to-day things like career, relationships and hobbies.

A simple rule I've come up with is: "If I have some activity or event I'm thinking about doing — and I'm 50/50 on it (with the alternative being just do nothing/stay at home, etc. — I try hard to choose to do the activity. I've never regretted making such a move. I do, however, regret some things I didn't do or simply doing nothing.

So, is there a...

- Business idea you want to pursue?

- A music CD/album you want to create?

- A book you want to pen?

I was so enamoured with these three things that old folks wished they'd done more of in life that for the first few weeks after I heard it, I used them as the outline for my To-Do List every day.

I'd write down:

- What legacy am I leaving?

- What time am I taking to reflect?

- What risks can I take!?

Listen to your elders!

5 Easy Ways To Increase Serendipity

I love serendipity — who doesn't? I met a mayoral candidate for San Francisco last year due to a certain something she and I each shared independently.

We all love serendipity — is it ever a negative thing?

You never hear someone say:

"That guy really stabbed me in the back — how serendipitous."

Right?

The layman's definition of serendipity is "happy accident" — the word serendipity is said to come from author Horace Walpole who played on the word Serendipity (an old name for Sri Lanka) used in a fairy tale called "The Three Princes Of Serendipity" about making discoveries by accident.

Here are the things I do to increase serendipity:

1) Send Out *Beacons* To Let Others Know You Exist

The most effective way to increase serendipity is to send out "beacons" — I first heard this mentioned by entrepreneur Jack Hidary in the book Power of Pull. Jack — who works on the neat iAmplify.com business with his brother Murray — uses the analogy of a ship at sea that sends out beacons to let others know where it is and where it's headed. Beacons — I like that.

Here are some examples of beacons I've used to increase serendipity:

Write A Blog

Most of the purpose of my Rob Kelly blog is to increase serendipity. I write about things that I feel I have some mastery over or that I want to learn about, and then I see who finds me.

I've met many people through my blog when they read my articles and then either send me a note through my Contact form or leave a comment at the bottom of this page. Here are a few people who've contacted me because of my blog postings:

- A guy with an awesome social media business plan (that he basically gave me to run with if I chose).

- A neat college student who wanted to help me any way he could just to get to know me better.

- An Israeli entrepreneur with a terrific Internet video business.

Leverage Social Networks (Facebook, LinkedIn, Twitter, etc.)

Other great "beacons" to use include Facebook (you can type your new interests in your "status"), LinkedIn (you can see who your connections hang out with) and Twitter. A venture capitalist named Joanna Rees began following me on Twitter and I looked up who she was (she had a blog!) and I found her background real intriguing.

That led to me to request a meeting with her at which she gave me the inside scoop that she was about to throw her hat in the ring to run for mayor of San Francisco (which she actively pursued!).

Type out stuff or follow people. And people like Joanna Rees might follow you.

Let People Know Where You're Hanging Out

I let people know some of the events I'm hanging out at, whether it's verbally, by email or through online tools like Facebook or Plancast.

Don't get me wrong — I don't telegraph where I am at every moment. But if I'm attending a public event, I put that out there so if someone wants to connect with me, they easily can.

Share Pictures & Videos

Perhaps you're more visual...words are not your thing. In that case, you could easily share pictures (through sites like Flickr or your own blog) and videos through your own blog or YouTube. If you do share pictures or videos, just remember to tag them properly so that others with similar interest can easily find you.

For example, you may be a photographer who has a really neat photo of the Golden Gate Bridge. In that case, you could share the picture (Flickr is an easy way to do that if you don't have your own blog/Web site) and make sure to title it "Golden Gate Bridge in the fog." — then, people searching Google for pictures of the Golden Gate Bridge (especially in the fog!) can easily find you. Sending out beacons = serendipity.

2) Be a "Go-Giver"

A simple way to increase your serendipity is to give, give, give — I like the corny term "go-giver" (versus go-getter) and wrote a piece about some tips on How To Be A Go-Giver that might stimulate some ideas. For example, I recently agreed to give some free business advice to entrepreneur Josh Schwarzapel, who was trying to build a cool new business that I had some experience in.

Josh returned the favor by introducing me to another entrepreneur (Kevin Gao of Hyperink) who then asked me to advise his new business. I would have never met the second entrepreneur if I hadn't helped the first one. I promise you this — if you go out and GIVE something/yourself to someone, you will increase the chances of "happy accidents." Serendipity!

3) Be More Of A "Connector" (Or At Least Hang Out With Them!)

One of the easiest ways to increase serendipity is to be a better connector. I'm a connector...and it's amazing how many opportunities connecting generates. I wrote in Why You Should Be Linkedin: Is $948 Per Connection Appealing!? about how valuable connections are and how to use LinkedIn to leverage that.

The easiest example of how to be a connector is to connect two people you know who you think can create special value together. The fun part is that those people you connect will credit you with the connection — and, if they're smart, they'll come back to you with opportunities for YOU!

Check out my article on Do These 3 Things And You'll Be A Much Better Networker on page 100 or How To Network Like A Top 500 Web Company CEO.

If you're looking for a good "connector" exercise check out How To Maximize The Number Of Valuable People You Meet In Life (The Connector Exercise). More connecting = more serendipity.

4) Write A Book (It's Easier Than It Sounds)

Writing a book is an amazing way to increase serendipity. I wrote a book a couple of years ago and I refer to it as my "100-Page Business Card" — I gave the book away for free to friends and family (and even some strangers) — and the opportunities that it generated continue to be simply amazing (that book was the nucleus for this book!).

You can print books for as little as $5 each and e-books are virtually free to distribute. The writing of a book can take some time, but you'd be surprised — some books are just 10,000 words these days. That could be the equivalent of just 10 to 20 blog postings!

Many people I've given the book to have sent fascinating people to meet with me, who were all helped by my book — a 100-page business card! Would you pay $5 (cost of printing the book) to have an incredible person walk into your life? I would. Writing a book = major serendipity.

5) Write Down Goals & Lists (The Law Of Attraction Really Works)

Anyone who knows me well knows that I love making lists of goals and projects. I believe that putting things in writing is one of the key first steps to making them a reality. If you don't know or believe me, check out The 10 [Maniacal] Steps I Take To Setting Goals or read one of many books about the Law Of Attraction (i.e: the Secret).

Last year I made a list of some CEOs I wanted to meet — one of them was a guy named Mitch Thrower who I had had a brief business encounter with when he was CEO of Active Network and I was leading a music startup called Mojam.

Mitch and I hadn't been in touch for years but I was impressed by some of the neat things he has done in his life (triathlons, authoring books, public speaking and his latest venture Bump Networks (enabling drivers to socialize with other drivers and businesses while driving- cool idea!).

I put Mitch on my "List Of CEOs To Connect With" and didn't think much of it for a while. Then, a couple of months ago, I was finishing up my workout at UCSF's gym in San Francisco and I noticed a small techie trade show going on in the hallway. As I walked by (in my sweaty outfit) I saw a booth for "Bump Networks" — I stopped and chatted with the guy manning the booth.

I said: "I once chatted with your founder...a guy named Mitch Thrower."

The booth rep beamed — he said: "I'm Mitch Thrower."

Mitch was really flattered I remembered him. We scheduled a call, caught up and found some mutual areas of interest. I'm not sure I would have noticed Bump's booth if I hadn't put Mitch's name on my "CEO List." Writing down your goals or lists of things you desire = more serendipity.

The "Campsite Rule"

Your mom or dad may have told you about the "Campsite Rule"...the part about leaving things as you found them—mine did. This goes for other people's things as well as your own.

For example, if you're staying at a friend's house, like I recently did with my ex-girlfriend, I had to think about this in terms of the linen on the bed. We had slept there for two nights and I certainly didn't want to leave the dirty linen there, but I also didn't know what the owners' preferences was in terms of washing linen.

While they were away they had a maid who was coming in and there was other dirty laundry sitting near the washer. We stripped the bed and made the bed so it looked as nice as when we found it. We put the linen in the washing machine (at least saving the maid one step). Then we left the owners a small gift of smoked fish in the kitchen.

We left their home better than we found it.

One of my favorite guests, the Moore family, recently stayed in my home and Kelly and Ted did a great job of leaving everything as they found it (this was no small feat seeing as they had two demolition sons – Brennan and Owen – with them!)

And, they left me with a gift of a new stack of To-Do stationary (I love lists!) Just think how much better life is when we all adhere to the "Campsite Rule" – just by leaving things as well if not better than we found them.

Assume Positive Intent

This is a tip I read from Indra Nooyi, the chairman & CEO of Pepsico, who is one of the top ranking women in terms of the size of business she runs, and she is of Indian descent running an American company – amazing! She says she learned this lesson from her father. Practicing this had an immediate impact on my day-to-day life.

One morning, for example, I was riding my bike back from yoga class around 8:45 a.m. and trying to make a left turn onto my street. There was both oncoming traffic and traffic behind me. I tried to slow down to turn, but there was too much traffic coming. Then, I tried to pause on my bike when a car came from behind me super fast, honked really loud and the driver began shouting at me.

It sent a shock through my body and my first impulse was to give the driver the finger or shout back. Instead, I assumed positive intent and imagined that the driver was just having a bad day and was probably a good guy who might even have

been looking out for me.

I pictured him going home to his apartment and perhaps having a tough life, one not as fortunate as mine, so I did nothing and let it go. Assuming positive intent calmed me down and I imagine, and hope, calmed him down a bit too!

"When Given The Choice of Being Right Versus Kind, Try Choosing Kind"

The above is one of my favorite quotes -- it's from Wayne Dyer who I first saw on PBS Television. He was 55 years old then and I found out later that he had been studying and teaching personal development for many years.

My personal development friend and former business partner, Eben Pagan, tells me that Wayne was one of his greatest influences. Wayne's quote:

"When given the chance of being right versus kind, try choosing kind," resonated with me.

After watching the rest of his TV show, I walked down the street to run an errand and someone walked right in front of me, abruptly cutting me off.

I was about to snicker and get upset when I remembered Wayne's quote.

Instead of making a snide remark to the man, I let him keep walking and said nothing. Who cares that I was right about being cut off? It was better to be kind and just let him keep going.

That made me feel good. I've been trying to practice being kind more than right ever since.

Practice Honesty

I hadn't heard these two words put together until I met Life Coach (and now friend) Terry Cranford in San Francisco.

It was also right around the time I was reading "Radical Honesty" by Brad Blanton, a radical book about – big surprise here – being honest!

I never considered myself to be dishonest, but a combination of things I learned from Coach Terry and the book made me appreciate that I was not being honest with myself or others.

I began journaling my acts of honesty (being honest with yourself is the first step). For example, I told myself that I drank a bit too much and that I didn't want to hang out with a particular friend. And then I began sharing honestly with others (being honest with others is the second step).

Here are some examples of acts of honesty:

- Admitting I made a stupid comment.

- Turning down a social invitation with the simple comment, "I feel like staying home tonight."

- Turning down an invitation by saying, "That's really not my cut of tea."

- Admitting that I had bad credit (now fixed – see my blog!).

- Admitting I am poor at handy work around the house.

- Admitting I was late because of poor time management.

- In general, mentioning the "Elephant in the room" (the thing that everyone is thinking but not saying)

The more honest I was, the better I felt!

Oh, and Mom, I have to admit that I am the one who scratched the side of Dad's old Jaguar when I was a teenager. Thank you in advance for forgiving me!

The Cool Secret Steve Jobs Asked My Friend Gary to Keep

Written October 5, 2011

I'm sad today, like millions of others, that the top inventor of our time, Steve Jobs, has died. I feel very lucky that I got to interview Steve Jobs for an article I wrote early in my career (I can remember how excited I got when he called me directly to chat about his startup, Next Computer, that he was struggling with!). I more recently got to ask Steve and Bill Gates a question about entrepreneurship (see Bill Gates, Steve Jobs & Me).

But, I have a cooler Steve Jobs item to tell you about. I want to share a story that Steve Jobs asked my friend Gary Brickman to keep secret years ago.

This is my old buddy Gary Brickman at CMP's/TechWeb's China Basin, San Francisco offices circa 1997 -- Steve Jobs asked him to keep a cool secret.

Gary was an incredible individual who was, among other things, a master of the early Internet and media (mostly at CMP Media/TechWeb) — he passed away June 26, 2000.

You should check out the cool site that was dedicated to him at GaryBrickman.com (thanks Matt Jalbert).

The Steve Jobs/Gary Brickman secret story is really rather simple. Gary suffered from brittle-bone disease, which left him in a wheel chair unable to use his legs. As you can see from the photo above, Gary had little problem using his hands (that's a marker he's tossing David Letterman style).

Anyway, Gary and Steve had some friends in common. Steve heard that Gary was having struggles with transportation — tough to get around in a car or bike without working legs! Steve bought him a van, fully equipped with gas and breaks that could be operated by hand.

Those who know Gary know that he was rarely found without the van close by. He practically lived in the thing. In fact, the first sign that Gary had died was that his van hadn't moved for a few days — and it wasn't like Gary to not be cruising around in it!

Anyway, the one condition Steve gave for buying Gary the van was that Gary wouldn't ever tell anyone that it was Steve Jobs who bought the van. Gary did tell me about it of course. And I'm now telling you. It's very cool to do something because it's the right thing to do...and not for public accolade.

Steve Jobs was cool...and so was Gary.

If Life is Too Easy, You Lose Your Joy

This Hopi Indian saying hits home for me. I find hard work to be one of the most rewarding things in life. In fact, the most rewarding experiences I have had were the hardest.

One example was when my close friend Howard "Howie" Burns died unexpectedly and the family asked friends to volunteer to speak at the service. Due to the unusual circumstances of Howie's death, no one agreed to speak. I was nervous about the idea of speaking but decided that if it were me being memorialized, I'd want someone stepping up.

So I volunteered. The preparation and the speech were among the hardest things I've ever done.

As I was called to the podium I was so nervous and scared that I was physically unable to make a sound with my voice. My mom or sister said something to me and I couldn't vocalize an answer. I thought I had lost my voice and wouldn't be able to give a speech for Howie.

But as I walked up the altar, my voice emerged and I was able to share a few stories about Howie. I'm sure glad I did, as no one else chose to speak. Can you imagine what a memorial service would be like if no one spoke?

As I walked out of the church, one of the deceased's family members (whom I never met) came up to me and said, "Thank you for speaking about Howie. There was so much more to him than most people knew and the stories you told about him were able to bring that to light!"

My heart filled. I knew I had done the right thing, and while difficult, it was one of the most rewarding experiences I've ever had.

The Hopi's were right. Life ain't always so easy but it's often the difficult things you do that bring you the most joy.

Gift Closet

For the first 35 years of my life I was horrible at getting gifts for people as I would wait to the last minute to try to find something. Well, that all changed when I began a "gift closet".

The gist of the gift closet is that I buy a gift every time it meets one of the following three criteria:

1. I want the item myself.

2. Someone I know would like the gift (even if it's not their birthday or a holiday).

3. Most people I hang out with would like the item.

My gift closet usually contains up to a dozen different gifts, and they have helped me out of a jam many a time! Some might say, "Well, isn't that impersonal to give a gift you bought without the recipient in mind?"

I say no! If these are quality items you are buying. Your quality friends and family will love them!

Note: I try to always have a bottle of champagne handy (room temperature) for a fall-back gift to bring to a party (or to use at my home to celebrate a spontaneous event!) Some smart person told me about that trick!

Donate To A Friend Every Time They Ask

I once heard my friend Matt Payne talking about donating money to a friend's cause and I asked him about it; his general philosophy is to donate money to any friend who asks.

I realized how simple yet powerful this is. First, it is rare that a friend asks me to donate money (perhaps a few times per year). Secondly, I can usually control the amount of money I donate (i.e. there is no minimum or it's pretty low) so it doesn't cost me much in the grand scheme of things.

As I did the math, I realized it's a relatively small financial commitment to donate money to a friend's cause every time they ask. It sure makes it simpler for me to decide and it of course helps a friend.

If you have ever asked someone for money, you know how difficult it can be. With this rule, you'll make it easier. Thanks Matt!

A Secret To Your Success At Anything: Help Those Around You Succeed

I didn't figure this one out until I was 37 years old and I opened up a chapter of a Jack Welch book on leadership. It mentioned that a good leader stops thinking about himself and just focuses on making those around him or her successful.

Well, I believe this applies not just to business, but to all of life. A fun test of this is to do something unconditional for a stranger, friend or co-worker and ask for nothing in exchange. See what happens next, it can be amazing!

I saw a guy around my neighborhood and he was always taking care of plants around Everett Middle School. I loved walking by the plants (which included many vegetables) and stopped him one day and asked him about the garden. It turned out that Larry The Landscaper did it all on his own simply through donations that he collected. Next time I saw Larry I handed him a decent-sized check as a donation.

Well, a few days later he stopped by my house with some old photos of the neighborhood (as a gift); they showed how the neighborhood looked 50 years ago. The following week he dropped off some tomatoes from the garden by his school; later he gave me a bunch of bok choy.

One day I had an indoor tree start dying on me and I realized through talking to experts that it was an outside plant. I gave it to Larry and he planted that tree near the front door of the school and nursed it back to health. All I did was help Larry succeed a little bit, and look at the multiple good things that happened!

Pay it Forward

I watched the Kevin Spacey movie Pay It Forward and was moved by it. I wept like a baby!

I took the movie kid's idea to heart and the next day handed a $20 bill to a homeless guy in our neighborhood asking him to accept it only if he could help two other people out with it.

I ran into him a few days later and asked him what he did with the $20. A huge smile appeared on his face and he told me he spent the $20 on taking out two heroin addict friends for some won-ton soup at our local Chinese restaurant.

He added that if he had merely handed them the cash (as opposed to buying them dinner) they would have bought heroin and shot it up.

I later came to know the homeless guy's name (Steve) and learned that he was an incredible individual who hit upon some hard luck.

Steve soon ended up getting cancer all over his body (he was too poor to treat any one part of it so it had spread).

Amazingly, he did the ultimate pay it forward. He sacrificed his body for some of the medical professionals at Stanford Hospital to help cure cancer. Pay it forward!

Passion &
Purpose

How To Write A Purpose Statement

In late 2007 I was introduced to "Coach Terry (Cranford)," a phone-based life coach. I was dubious about the phone-only part but I gave it a shot for a few months and learned a ton.

The most important thing I learned from Terry was the importance of having a statement of purpose for anything substantial in my life.

I began writing a statement of purpose for my life, my business, my role in business, a holiday trip, my romantic relationship or even just my plan for a day.

I've found it useful to constantly be asking myself what the purpose of something I'm doing is, or when people ask me to do something or say they are doing something, I ask them: "What is the purpose of that?"

Be purposeful about all things in your life…and you'll find that the outcome is more favorable. So, here's how to write a statement of purpose along with some purpose statement tips:

1) List Your Expectations

Write down all the expectations you have about your purpose related to a certain topic (e.g. your life, job, relationship with someone, etc.) on the left-hand side of the page. Examples of expectations are wants, needs and even fears — for example, if you're writing a purpose statement about a job you should be answering the following questions:

What do I really <u>want</u> my job to be?

What do I really <u>need</u> in my job?

What <u>fears</u> do I have about my job?

Spend at least 5 to 10 minutes on this part...and really open up! You should now have at least 7 to 10 expectations — and they will probably be centered around a few topics or themes (e.g. for a job, it might be to make money, have fun, have a flexible schedule, etc.)

2) Purpose Statement

Now, fresh from writing out those expectations, immediately write down one long sentence that starts with "The purpose of my _____ is to ..." and the rest of the statement should flow pretty naturally (*hint: if you have any challenge here, take your expectations and group them into a few topics or themes and use those as your purpose statement*). Writing a purpose statement is that easy!

You now have the beginnings of the purpose statement — you can refine this now or later (if you're like me, you'll find that you remember new wants, needs and fears later on — so just add them in and iterate).

3) Write "I Will" Statements

Return to the expectations list and to the right of each of them write down an "I will" statement. The "I will" statement should be something actionable that you could do to be more purposeful.

Try to make each "I will" statement specific, measureable, actionable and timely. Don't worry about ever doing such things — this isn't a to-do list — just write it down! The act of merely writing them down will make you more mindful of your purpose.

I promise you that if you do this exercise, you will be more purposeful on whatever the topic. So, now you have a purpose statement (remember, you can refine it all you want) and even some actions that you can take (I sometimes DO treat it like a to-do list by printing it out and doing some of the actions immediately)

Samples of Purpose Statements

Here are some sample purpose statements I've written:

Life Purpose Statement — My life purpose is to positively vibrate the Universe through friends, family and even strangers.

Purpose Statement For Layoffs I Had To Make — The purpose of our layoffs is to be able to execute the plan on a timely basis, to be respected in the execution and to protect the jobs of productive people.

Business Purpose Statement — The purpose of our business is to have fun, help people and make a little money.

Purpose Statement For My Job – The purpose of my job is to make money, meet only with people I love and respect, work on things I enjoy and provide a flexible schedule to take care of the primary choices in my life.

Purpose Statement For A New Management Meeting I Had To Start (see my Daily Huddle Article) — The purpose of the daily huddle meeting is to align the management team and to increase the speed of our growth.

Purpose Statement For My Wife — The purpose of the relationship with my life-mate is to have a passionate, healthy and positive relationship (while still enjoying some vices!) — which leads to a larger family with children I adore.

Or you can follow the advice personal development guru Steve Pavlina who gave these steps from How To Write A Purpose Statement article:

1. Write at the top of a document, "What is my true purpose in life?"

2. Write an answer (any answer) that pops into your head. It doesn't have to be a complete sentence. A short phrase is fine.

3. Repeat step 3 until you write the answer that makes you cry. This is your purpose.

Enjoy being purposeful!

3 Simple Steps To Help You Pursue Your Passion

Steve Jobs told Stanford students in 2005:

"..for the past 33 years, I have looked in the mirror every morning and asked myself: 'If today were the last day of my life, would I want to do what I am about to do today?' And whenever the answer has been 'No' for too many days in a row, I know I need to change something."

Jobs is talking about passion. Well, a goal in my life is to help people explore their passions, ideally in a way that helps them make a living.

I thought I'd share three steps that I used to further my own career passions. Ok, so let's dig in...

Step 1: Pick a Passion

It starts with picking a passion — your passion may be obvious to you (politics, sports, medicine, photography religion) and you're good to go. If your passions are not obvious to you, ask those closest to you (friends, colleagues, family members) what they think.

If you still don't know, here are two good questions to ask yourself:

1. What is it that you do where time just slips away?

2. What would you attempt if you knew you could not fail? (a great question that Dr. Robert Scuhller once posed and Tony Robbins made famous)

For me, I picked the subject of business (that's what I know) and in particular business advice (like much of the content found in this blog).

Step 2: Deposit Yourself/Content Into The Universe

Your next step is to put yourself or, more specifically, your content out there. I call these bits of content "beacons" or "knols" that you're putting out into the Universe. I'm talking about journaling...but not any old journal (although that's better than nothing)– you need to start a blog!

The reason for a blog is that it allows you to receive feedback — more on that in step 3 below. As far as blogging tools, I recommend WordPress...it's free and effective (check out my "7 Easy Steps On How To Set Up A Blog Using WordPress" article)

Producing Content (i.e writing)

So now you start creating content. There are three types of content you can start with depending on what you're comfortable with/best at:

- Text — If you're a good writer, focus your blog on text

- Audio — If you've got an amazing radio voice (I don't), utilize audio

- Video — If you're very visually enticing (again, I'm not), pick video

You're going to want to contribute content to your blog consistently (at least a few times a week)...some tips:

1) Re-use existing knols of content such as:

- Emails you write to friends or colleagues about the topic you're passionate about

- Presentations/Speeches you've given on your topic

- Papers you wrote for school

- Opinions you have on other people's articles/videos you consume

2) Don't' worry about being perfect – you can always go back and correct something.

3) Be specific (more on that later)

Step 3: Get Feedback

There are three types of feedback you're going to want to get:

Feedback #1: Web Analytics

For this, I recommend you set up Google Analytics (read this 3 Easy Steps To Using Google Analytics that I wrote, which includes a great video!) — Google Analytics is free and easy to use.

Google Analytics will tell you things such as:

- How many visitors you receive

- Which geographic areas they come from

- Which other Web sites link to your site

- And a whole lot more

Remember how I told you earlier to be specific in your content? Well, Google and its Google Analytics loves when you're specific — they will tell you how many people arrived at your blog through Googling a specific keyword. Here are examples of how specific the search terms can be from people who searched Google and ended up here at my blog:

- "Best name for a Web site to attract customers"

- "Process of converting a bridge loan into a term loan"

- "Macy's credit card turned down my application, why? Fico score over 800"

The more specific the better!

Feedback #2: Set Up A Comment system

This allows you to hear what people think about your content. It's really fun to get real people talking to you. And anyone who takes the time to comment on your blog is someone who could be a customer, partner or even friend.

Comments are fairly standard in WordPress blogs you set up, but make sure to pay attention to it (especially moderating the comments, as you may get some spam, and replying back to commenters).

Feedback #3: Set Up An Affiliate Program (To Get Customer Feedback)

What is an affiliate program you may ask? Basically, it allows you to sell other people's products and receive a commission (Read the Affiliate Marketing Programs: Tips From A Veteran Q&A I did with a colleague). The best example of an affiliate program is Amazon's – they allow you to easily link to products that they sell and receive around 4% to 8% commissions if anyone clicks through to Amazon and buys something.

It's tough to get rich from affiliate marketing (5% of a $20 book you link to only gets you $1 in commissions) (read this Myths of Blogging I wrote) ......but it is super-useful to get a sense of what types of things your readers like to buy. Ideas for Amazon products that might be related to your blog topic include:

- Books

- Movies

- Shoes

- Jewelry

- Hobby products

Ah-Hahs

What were some "ah-hahs" from my blog experience...and how did it help me develop my passion? Well, I chose to write about business as I mentioned. Here's some feedback I received:

The Content That's Most Popular With Your Readers May Surprise You:

I wrote about Personality Types in business (80% of my traffic came from about just 15% of my postings (those postings took me just a weekend and I have blogged 120 other postings and no other articles came close in volume) (read Pareto's 80/20 rule). That led to me to create TopTypes.com, an entirely new website.

Your Readers Buy More Than Just The Products You Write About

I sold 14 different types of products; half of the sales were items I never wrote about (Amazon gives you credit for whatever they buy once they click your link (for that visit). They included:

- 50 Books

- 2 Beauty products

- 1 Grocery product (Latte Drink mix)

- 1 Health product

- 2 Home and Garden

- 1 Piece of jewelry

- 8 Kindle eBooks

- 2 Kitchen products

- 1 MP3 Download

- 1 Office product

- 1 Pair of shoes

- 2 Sports

- 1 Toy

- 12 Videos on Demand

The most practical thing I learned is that one of the most popular keywords people search on that leads to a visit to my blog is "Careers." I had never thought of careers as being a topic that I was much of an authority on, but clearly Google disagrees and sends much of the Web universe searching careers my way.

In fact, I began coaching more people on their careers after that and realized I do enjoy it.

Final thoughts: If you follow the 3-step plan above I think you'll make enormous gains in understanding what career passions to pursue. It's not easy, but it's worth it.

Increase Your Confidence Through The "Qualities of Achievement" Exercise

Most of us can use a confidence boost once in awhile. Here's one exercise I used that works...and it actually feels good and positive as you're doing it! I call it the..."Qualities of Achievement Exercise"

Step 1: Write Down Your Major Achievements In Life

Write down the achievements in life that you're really proud of — it can be related to business, family, sports or anything.

What's important about the achievements you select is that it made you feel really good.

Here are examples of achievements I'm proud of:

- Winning the championship at a basketball tournament in Fire Island (pictured above)

- Moving to San Francisco from New York (which I decided spontaneously with my then-girlfriend in a NY cafe)

- Founding a start-up

- Playing guitar onstage with my buddy Larry at his wedding reception (see picture below)

Note: You should keep a log of these achievements somewhere as these are what your life is really all about (I keep them at the top of my goals document (please see page 50 for The 10 Maniacal Steps I Take To Setting Goals).

Step 2: Select One Achievement & Write Down The Qualities You Possessed For The Achievement

To the right of the achievement, write down the qualities you possessed (or conditions you set up) to make that achievement happen. For example, to win the basketball championship I wrote down things like:

- I practiced 3 times a week (aka 'created a ritual')

- I focused on my strengths (aka 'unique abilities')

- I was a team player

- I gave it everything I had

- I was in good physical shape

It helps to write these down as "I [fill in the blank]" statements. You should have at least 5 to 10 of these qualities.

Ok, you should be feeling pretty good about yourself at this point…after all, you're revisiting some amazing achievement from your life! That was a great day, wasn't it!?

So, let's do another achievement (you'll later see that it's important to do multiple achievements).

Step 3: Write Down A Second Achievement & List Out The Qualities/Conditions

Step 4: Write Down A Third Achievement & Do The Same

Step 5: Create Your Master List Of Qualities Of Achievement

Now that you've done 3 achievements, you should have a list of a couple of dozen qualities listed. Review the list on the right-hand side (the reasons you accomplished these achievements) as this is your master list of "Qualities of Achievement" — some of the many things you possess to do amazing things.

There will be qualities that repeat among achievements too — even though you may use slightly different language for them — those repeat qualities are arguably among the most powerful qualities you possess! I found it useful to make a separate list (mine is below) of the repeating qualities. Here are some of my own:

- I utilized my network of contacts

- I was bold

- I focused

- I bought time

- I was positive

- I leveraged my unique abilities

- I created a plan

- I did the "right thing"

- I was persistent

- I practiced

- I created rituals

- I was persuasive

Step 6: Whip Out Your Qualities Of Achievement Any Time You Need A Confidence Boost

Now, what's cool is that any time you are facing some new endeavor, you can look at your 'Qualities of Achievement List" to be reminded of the qualities YOU possess to further achieve!

Furthermore, these qualities will give you ideas on how to tackle your new achievement! After all, you achieved greatness before...and you will surely achieve it again!

7 Ugly Reasons Your Ideas Don't Turn Into Reality

"Ideas are like @$$holes…," my friend Ralph Clark once said:

"…everyone has one!" Ralph's gonna hate me for mentioning that one! You hear it almost every day: "I have an idea for a new product…or a new Web site." Perhaps you even say it yourself.

An idea I borrowed from Chris Dixon is to keep new business ideas in a spreadsheet.

But most often the idea dies right there…or, worse, you hear someone whine or brag about the idea later when someone ELSE has turned it into a product. "Hey, I thought up a car sharing service just like Zipcar five years ago!"

If you want to avoid being one of those idea-snobs, here are 7 mistakes to avoid when you have an idea that you want to turn into a reality

1) You Keep Your Idea A Secret

Many people keep their ideas a secret — they don't share it with anyone. This is probably the worst mistake you can make. This may be because you are worried someone will steal the idea or because you fear failure or lack confidence.

I suggest that you keep your ideas in a journal. I use Google Docs to keep my ideas (and ideas of friends) and I rate them usually on a scale of 1 to 10 based on:

- How much capital I have to put at risk to test the idea

- How much financial upside the idea has

- How confident I am in the business model of the idea

- How close the business idea is to my core competencies

- How consistent the idea is with my values

- How fun the idea is

- How I use a formula to determine their yield

And I can pull up the pipeline of ideas any time on my iPhone.

2) You're Afraid Your Idea Will Fail

People are unwilling to face the fear of failure. As Master Yoda famously said:

"Fear is the path to the dark side. Fear leads to anger. Anger leads to hate. Hate leads to suffering."

For some more inspirational words on conquering fear, check out these Fear Quotes.

3) You Don't Take Action On Your Idea

"Good thoughts are no better than good dreams, unless they can be executed." – Ralph Waldo Emerson.

The #1 cure for failure, in my opinion, is simply taking action…any action! As teacher Dale Carnegie once said:

"Action breeds confidence and courage. If you want to conquer fear, do not sit home and think about it. Go out and get busy!" If you want some more words of inspiration, check out my Action Quotes article.

4) You Lack Confidence In Your Idea

Oh, man, low confidence can crush any idea…and quickly! There are some great ways to boost confidence including this Confidence Building Exercise that includes my fun Qualities of Achievement (page 41).

5) You Don't Use Advisors To Develop Your Idea

People who have ideas need to have an advisor or two around them who know a bit about the topic of the idea (or at least execution of ideas in general).

This may be a colleague, sibling, parent, child or friend. Search LinkedIn or Facebook for keywords related to your idea to see who you know. And if you still haven't formed much of a social network yet, check out the Business Networking section of my blog for a bunch of free tips. People love to give advice…so take it!

After you've shared an idea with an advisor or two, you need to get broader feedback on it. One tip I give friends is to start tweeting about it on Twitter or, better yet, write about your idea in a blog. You might check out step 3 of my article on 3 Simple Steps To Help You Pursue Your Passion to get some tips on putting yourself out there and getting feedback through a blog.

I prefer setting up my own blog because you can get set up Google Analytics on it - for instance, I can see that the most popular search terms on my blog include "mission statement" and "alliteration."

Check out the 3 Easy Steps To Using Google Analytics if you want to try it out on a Web site you have access to. You'll be amazed at what serendipity can get created through putting yourself out there AND getting feedback on it.

7) You & Your Idea Lack An "Accountability Buddy"

To execute an idea you need what I call an "accountability buddy" – this is someone who will hold you accountable for testing out your idea into a reality. For example, you can ask them to have a monthly phone call or meeting with you in which you update them on your progress of turning the idea into a reality. Perhaps you can hold them accountable on one of their ideas too!

Getting Results

The 10 Maniacal Steps I Take For Setting Goals

"Your goals, minus your doubts, equal your reality." – Ralph Marston

It took me 40 years to figure out that the key to life is feeling like I had a fulfilling day — I accomplish that through setting goals – I've set so many goals that I've identified nine groups of them (the ones I've written on these stones and drift-wood I found on the beaches of New Zealand!).

I believe that without goals your progress comes to a screeching halt. As Ralph Marston of The Daily Motivator once said.

"Here's how I set my goals: I define what I want in my entire life and then chunk down my goals from there. "

This is inspired by one of Stephen Covey's 7 Habits of Highly Successful People: "begin with the end in mind"

Note: I keep my goals document in Google Docs and I include a list of my proudest achievements (the ones I mentioned in Qualities Of Achievement on page 41) at the top of the doc– aren't goals simply more achievements you want to make that you'll be proud of!?

1) Start With Your Life Purpose Statement

The first thing I do is write a life purpose statement – follow the easy steps for that on page 32. For example, my life purpose statement is "To positively vibrate the Universe through friends, family and even strangers."

2) Write Down Your "Big Picture Goals"

After that, I started to notice that there are a handful of really important "big picture goals." These are the more specific items that I know will support my life purpose statement above.

Here is an example of my big picture goals:

1. Love many (incl. serving others in need)

2. Be loved by many

3. Create legacy (leave the world much better off than I found it)

4. Improve my family

5. Have many close friends with whom I stay in touch

6. Create & grow businesses

7. Feel healthy-good

8. Express myself creatively (through books, movies, music, art, etc.)

9. See the world

10. Connect with nature

3) Write Down Your "Lifetime Goals"

Now you're ready for a more specific list of "lifetime goals" that will support your "big picture goals."

Examples of my lifetime goals include to:

- Have an amazing wife

- Have children

- Become closer to my immediate family

- Have friends in multiple places and with whom I enjoy being

- Create multiple businesses

- Write a book

- Record a CD/album

- Create a movie

- Live to 110

- Have substantial impact on the education system

- Have substantial impact on curing pancreatic cancer

- Advance my local community

- Spend 30 days per year overseas

- Have a net worth of let's call it $1 billion (that's a fun # for this exercise!)

4) Set Your 20-Year Goals

Then, I set more specific 20-year goals that will support those lifetime goals. For example, here are some of mine:

- Have a happy wife

- Have 2+ children

- Have formed a (bi-)annual family trip tradition

- Have formed a tradition of a get-together with my Chicago friends

- Have formed a tradition of a get-together with my high school friends

- Have participated in 20 businesses

- Have five businesses sold or producing cash for me

- Be the healthiest 63-year-old I know!

- Have a net worth of...let's call it $100 million

5) Set Your 5-Year Goals

Then I set five-year goals that will support my 20-year goals such as:

- Get married

- Attempt to have children

- Have five family vacations

- Have five to 10 trips with Chicago and high school friends combined

- Participate in five real businesses

- Have one business producing substantial cash flow

- Have a net worth of $100 million

Then do the same with:

Set Your 1-Year Goals

Your 1-year goals should support your 5-year goals.

Set Your 90-Day Goals

Your 90-day goals should support your 1-year goals.

Set Your 30-Day Goals

Your 30-day goals should support your 90-day goals.

Now, I keep all of the above in a Google Doc and I print out the 90 day and 30 day goals and keep it on my desk in a stand-up binder.

9) Set Your Weekly Goals

I set my weekly goals every Sunday night with an emphasis on the 5 or so major projects in my life that I want to make progress on to support my 30-day goals.

10) Set Your Daily Goals

Every night before I go to sleep I write down my daily goals for the next day (to support my weekly goals).

Lately, I'm borrowing something I heard Marc Andreessen does with his daily goals: he attempts to do 3 major things each day (I'm always testing/refining such approaches to goal-setting)

Revising Goals

I revise my goals periodically as I add, delete or modify what I want to try to do in life. Don't worry about missing some goals. You're still achieving way more than if you hadn't set the goals at all! In fact, once thing you will find is that you will achieve some things that weren't even goals at all...those are bi-product achievements as a result of your goal setting.

What I Write Down Every Night Before I Go To Sleep

Finally, right before I'm going to go to sleep, I write down the handful of awesome things that I accomplished or experienced that day. It's usually just a few bullets of stuff. They won't necessarily be directly related to my goals — they'll just be things that make me feel great.

5 Steps To Making Your Outcomes Inevitable (aka "Inevitability Thinking")

I remember when my friend Eben Pagan shared the concept of Inevitability Thinking with me — it's such a simple yet powerful approach to achieving your objective…damn, why didn't I think of that!?

The easiest way for me to share Inevitability Thinking is to give an example (I'm going to use a hypothetical example of an Internet business I want to build).

To do this exercise on your own you would need:

- A Calculator

- Google

- Your Brain

- A half-hour or so of time

But, if you want, you can just read my version of this exercise first. Ok, so here are the steps:

1) Articulate Your Objective

First step is to articulate your objective. For this exercise, let's assume your objective is to build a content-based Web site that generates $20,000 per month in advertising revenue. Sound good?

2) Identify Your Time Frame?

Easy next step: let's pick a time period to meet your objective of $20,000 in ad revenue per month.

We all want to reach our goals immediately...but let's be realistic: how does one year sound? After all, most things that matter in life take time. One year it is!

3) List Your Inevitability Levers To Achieving Your Objective

Ok, this is still super-easy. Now you just identify what levers to pull to make it imperative to achieving your objective.

I call these inevitability levers because they are imperative to your objective. Let's start at the very top-line of levers you'll be working with. For example, to build a content-based Web site that generates ad revenue, you're going to need at least these two levers:

A) Advertisements (that are sold)

B) Content (that's on your Web site)

Note: Down below we'll drill down deeper into a few mini-levers within these inevitability levers.

4) Make Realistic/Conservative Assumptions Quantifying Your Inevitability Levers

You do have to get your hands a little dirty on this one. Next up, you're going to start to make assumptions about your inevitability levers.

The key tip about your assumptions is to make them realistic/conservative: after all, we're trying to make it INEVITABLE that you'll achieve your objectives (don't be overly optimistic). Let's start with your advertisements

Assumptions on Selling Advertisements

Advertising revenue is a pretty simple formula: you've got to price your ads and you've got to sell your ads. Let's start with ad pricing: what's a conservative assumption we can use on how much you can make from an online advertisement?

Shh, here's a secret tip on how to track that down: go to a site called "Google.com." I searched "average CPM (CPM stands for cost per thousand impressions) of an online ad" and I found that $2.43 is a good average CPM for the Internet as a whole, according to Comscore.

Note: I also found a cool graph in this Adify Report that showed CPMs for different vertical markets such as automotive, beauty/fashion, business, moms and parents, sports, technology, travel, real estate, healthy living/lifestyle, news and food. The CPMs in this graph were much higher (average of $7.71 but you want your objectives to be inevitable so lets be conservative and use the $2.43 figure instead).

Ok, let's use the average CPM of $2.43; if we use that, then that means you'll generate $2.43 for every 1,000 impressions (aka page views) of your Web site. To keep things simple, let's assume that you're just selling one ad on every page of your Web site.

5) Start Asking Inevitability Questions

Now we need to figure out how much volume of ads you need to sell (since we're selling one ad per page, we can just call what we're looking for: "page views" (i.e. each time someone views a page of your content, one ad is served).

Now, bust out your calculator: you want $20,000 per month so you're going to have to do the following calculation to figure out what would make it inevitable to get enough page views to generate twenty grand:

20,000 ÷ by ($2.43/1000) = 8,230,452 page views that you would need to generate $20,000 in ad revenue.

Ok, now you have to do the same exercise with 8.23M page views: What would make it inevitable that you would generate 8.23M page views? A certain number of "visits" to your Web site. On the Internet, a page view is generated by a visitor visiting your site and looking at a certain number of pages.

Ok, back to assumptions (and don't forget to be conservative about your assumptions…after all, we're trying to make it inevitable that you'll achieve your objective!). And don't put your calculator away just yet either!

Visitor Assumptions

So we need to use another assumption for how many pages a visitor would view to continue our math. You can go Google your particular vertical, but let's keep things simple and assume that a conservative estimate is that an average visitor will view 5 pages each time they visit your site.

Calculator-time again:

So, if you want it to be inevitable to generate 8.23M page views, then you would need to do this calculation: 8.23M ÷ 5 = 1,646,000 visits

So, if you had 1.65M visits it would be inevitable that you would generate 8.23M page views and thus $20,000 in ad revenue (using your conservative assumptions of course!). Ok, so now you might ask: How the heck am I gonna get 1.65M visitors to my Web site (in a month!)!?

Well, you're probably already thinking of a few different ways such as:

- Buying Ads

- Appearing on Oprah

- Getting Sites to Link to You

All are good approaches and you could apply inevitability thinking to any of them...but let's keep it simple. Let's say you believe that your Web site's content can help you attract traffic (remember, content IS your other core lever!).

Content Assumptions

Ok, so how much content would you need to make it inevitable that you would attract 1.65M visitors per month? Ok, you're going have to make some more assumptions...this time around content.

Here's where I use my trusty SEOBook tool (see How To Have X-Ray Vision About Your Competition) which will tell me both:

- Number of Visitors To Different Sites

- Number of Pages of Content (at least according to Google & Yahoo whose job it is to index pages on the Web)

Let's say that you find that on average your competition generates 100 visitors per month for each page of content that they have (by the way, an example of one page of content would be this article you're reading right now).

Calculator-time again!

So, if you want it to be inevitable that you'll receive 1.65M visits in a month through content then you'd do the following calculation: 1.65M ÷ 100 = 165,000 pages of content that you would need

Ok, I know, it sounds like a lot of content. But, remember, this is one year from now. And, actually, there are tons of Web sites who generate hundreds of thousands of pages of content with little cost (beyond engineering time and hosting cost).

They get their voluminous content from users (aka "user-generated content") and many of them do it merely by providing a quality bulletin board or question and answer service. Check out StackOverflow, for example:

SEOBook tells me they have 8 million pages indexed by Google (note: they were founded in 2000 so they've been doing this for 10 years)...and they provide this primarily through offering a Q&A service for engineers.

StackOverFlow claims more than 1M visitors every month...now we're talking! Ok, so now what would make it inevitable that you generated 165,000 pages of content? Well, let's assume for the moment that you're going to do a blog instead to generate your content.

Conservation Assumptions Again:

Let's assume that you can write 3 blog entries a day or about 1,000 per year (I'm giving you a couple of weeks of vacation time!)...well, to get to 165,000 pages of content that would take you 165 years!

The oldest living man right now is only 114 so let's go to plan B. Well, there are actually free multi-user blogging platforms that allow you to let others blog beyond just you!

So, let's assume that you can get other writers like you to post 3 blog entries per day (around 1,000 per year with a few vacation days for them too (you're no slave-driver!).

So, to get 165,000 pages of content through multi-user blogging then you would need: 165,000 ÷ 1,000 = 165 Blog Writers

Ok, so now what would make it inevitable that you could sign up 165 blog writers. Perhaps you have a bunch of Facebook friends or alumni or colleagues who you could talk into helping you blog. But that would be tough for most people.

Did I Mention You'll Have To Google A Few Things In This Exercise?

Let's look around for a writers group…Googling "writers group" gives me WriterMag, a magazine with more than 30,000 writers. Ok, so what would it take for you to convince 160 of those 30,000 writers (.533% of them) to write for your blog (many writers might do it for free just for publicity!).

Let's assume that you talked to WriterMag's ad sales team and they told you that they were super-confident that if you ran a full-page black and white ad in their magazine — offering their 30,000 readers free publicity on your blog — every month for six months that it would be inevitable that you would get your 160 bloggers.

Well, such an ad looks like it would cost about $10,000 according to the rate card on their Web site (you can often get discounts to "rate card" and my guess is that you'd get at least 25% off for a 6-month commitment (times are tough for the publishing industry!).

So, a commitment by you of $7,500 should get you the 6 months of full-page ads. The gist of this inevitability thinking exercise is that:

- If you bought $7,500 worth of ads you could get

- 160 bloggers to create…

- 160,000 pages of content that would generate…

- 1.65M visits per month, which would produce…

- 8.23M page views per month, which could be sold for

- $2.43 CPM, which would make you

- $20,000 per month in advertising sales...

- in one year's time

This is of course a simplified version of how you'd really conquer your objective (the devil will be in the details and you're going to have to do your homework on levers, assumptions and the approaches you use).

But the point is: if your levers and assumptions are roughly correct, you will roughly achieve your objective through this approach. I hope you found this inevitability thinking exercise useful. Thanks, Eben!

How To Get A Win-Win Result From A Tough 50/50 Decision

A family friend asked for career advice the other day — he was trying to make a decision between finding a new job or staying put at his current job.

He was torn — almost manic — about which way to go…so I busted out the "Win-Win" exercise inspired by Yogi/Life Coach Terry.

I like using the "Win-Win Exercise" for making tough decisions — when the choice seems to be close to 50/50 — because you can literally get the best of both worlds…a true "win-win."

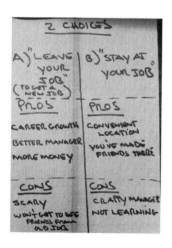

This Decision-Making exercise is easy: list off the pros and cons of your two choices (e.g. my friend is deciding between leaving his job or staying at his job.). And then there's a cool twist on the next page!

Step 1: List The Two Choices At The Top Of A Page

In this case, my friend was making a decision between these two choices:

A) Leave his job (To get a new job)

B) Stay at his job (Which has been crappy)

Write those down at the top of a page (one on the left and one on the right) (like in the image on page 63).

Step 2: List Out The Pros And Cons Of Each

I know what you're thinking: "Is this just another lame pros and cons exercise?" No, this is much cooler! Now you list the pros and cons below each choice.

Ok, so my friend's pros (for Choice A (leaving his job)) were:

- Career growth

- Finding a better manager

- Making more money

Cons for Choice A were:

- It's scary (to leave his job)

- He won't get to see his friends from his old job as often

Then we did the same with Choice B (in this case "stay at your job").

Pros:

- Convenient location (San Francisco (where he lives!))

- He's made friends there (at his current job)

Cons:

- He has a crappy manager (she sounds like she truly sucks)

- He's not learning much (again, crappy manager)

Step 3: Immediately Do A Gut Check On Which Choice Feels Right

Now that you've listed out the pros and cons of each choice, right then and there listen to your gut (and heart) on what **FEELS** like the right decision. Don't worry about being wrong! Just pick one...if you're wrong, it'll still work out!

If you're really scared about this, then read what Bruce Lee and others advise in 14 Quotes To Help You Overcome Your Fear. In the case of my friend, it was clear that his gut was telling him to go for Choice A: to leave his job! Right on!

Step 4: Focus On The Pros Of Both Choices (To Make A True "Win-Win")

Ok, now that you have decided that you're leaning towards once choice – e.g. my friend wants to leave his job — I want you to cross out the cons from both choices. That's right, cons suck...you don't want them...they are for losers who don't take action (check out my 13 Quotes To Help Kick Your Ass Into Gear).

Now take out another piece of paper and write the name of the choice you chose along with just the pros from both choices.

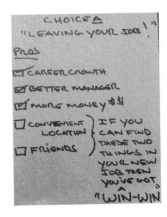

The key of the win-win exercise is to capture the best of both worlds: the pros of the choice your gut tells you to go with AND the pros of the choice you're not making.

Step 5: Look At The Pros From The Choice You Didn't Make (And Make Them Happen!)

So now my friend has his pros from both choices as:

1. Career growth

2. Better manager

3. More money

4. Convenient location

5. Friends he made from his old job (which I now just call "Friends")

Since you already know you're going to get the first three pros in your new job, then you simply have to focus on the two other pros from the choice you didn't make. In my friend's case, this is relatively easy:

Convenient location — He wants to keep working in San Francisco so he just needs to focus his new job search on San Francisco.

Friends — This is trickier but easily doable: He made good friends at his old job so he's got to commit himself to keeping in touch with his favorite friends from that old job now that he won't be seeing them day to day.

And, of course, he should embrace the fact that he will make new friends at his new job. He left our meeting confident that he should go for the new job and that he would nail all 5 pros. He had a true win-win.

My favorite part of this exercise is that my friend could have chosen Choice B: Staying put at his job...and we could have done the same exercise to get him a win-win — although it would be a bit more work since we'd have to move him away from his crappy manager!

To Get Your Desired End Result, Reverse-Engineer These 5 Easy Steps

I sat down in the Palm Springs hotel suite of T. Harv Eker, best-selling author of Secrets Of The Millionaire Mind and he shared a philosophy on how to get what you want in life that really resonated with me.

It applies to any results such as getting a new job, a new car, a better relationship and improved health. The philosophy is to reverse-engineer the process of what you want.

T.Harv goes way more into depth in his books and seminars, and much may have been lost in translation and brainstorming, but here is the gist of what I remembered from the chat.

T. Harv said (and I'm paraphrasing):

"So, you want results first, right? Well, what leads to results? That would be (taking) action. So what leads to action? Well, that would be having a feeling about something (feeling strongly enough to take action)."

"What leads to feeling something? That would be thinking about something. Finally, what leads to thinking about something? Well, that would be what I call programming (what you were taught as a child, how you see the world)."

T. Harv. said that most people think more about the end-game (e.g. taking action or even just the end result itself) than they do about the earlier, higher-leverage items such as programming, thinking and feeling.

Let me give you my own example:

If the end-result you want are to buy an expensive car, yet you were taught (programmed) by mom or dad that possessing an expensive car was a bad thing (because it flaunted wealth), then it will be very difficult for you to acquire your new car by simply taking action.

Your feelings about the car may be very mixed because of your parents' influence and you may not be able to talk openly to people about wanting a new car even if you want it.

If that's your case, here's how to reverse engineer the process:

1) Programming

Decide that you disagree with your parents about their thoughts on expensive cars. This may sound easy but deciding that you disagree with a value that a parent taught is a big deal, so you start there.

2) Thinking (and Talking)

Continue to think about the car and all the details surrounding it (color, feel of leather interior, price, etc.).

T. Harv. didn't mention this, but I consider "talking"about your desires to be key here – afterall, talking is just an extension of thinking (thinking is a dialogue with yourself and talking is a dialogue with another). So talk about the new car you want with those around you!

3) Feeling:

You will begin to feel more inspired about the car. You will literally, as they say in sports, be "feeling it."

4) Taking Action:

You will now be more likely to "kick the tires" of that car you want, you'll take action through a test drive.

5) Results

You will get that new car!

My Annual Income Doubled Every Time I Did One Of These 4 Things

As I mentioned in the *"5 C's"*, compensation is key to your career.

Towards that end, I plotted my compensation over the last 22 years (graph below) to figure out what caused it to go up (and down).

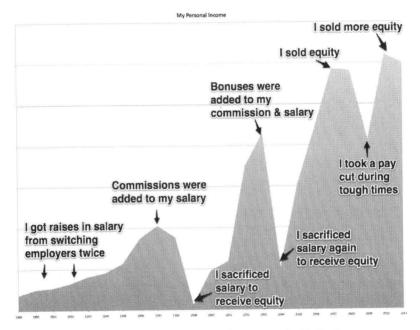

Above is my income data from 1989 to the present (with the income (exact amounts hidden) in the vertical axis and the years in the horizontal axis).

The key takeaways on what caused my pay increases were:

1) Joining A New Company

In my early years, the main way my pay increased was when I joined a new company. They tended to give me a higher salary just to join them.

2) Commissions

My compensation increased when I agreed to take on a role that offered both salary and commissions.

This was the first time I made any money beyond salary. I loved it because my commissions were calculated based on metrics I needed to hit (i.e. revenue objectives).

3) Bonuses

Similarly, in one role I was able to participate in a bonus program that, like commissions, paid me when I reached certain goals. This increased my compensation.

4) Equity

Finally, as I began to take more senior roles at companies I had the opportunity to add equity (i.e. stock) as part of my compensation.

I was able to sell this equity later on which increased my income.

Note: I did have to sacrifice my salary to get in the position to obtain equity, but this was worth it for my long-run compensation.

What If I'm Not Eligible For Commissions, Bonus Or Equity?

I believe that everyone has the opportunity to increase their pay through non-salary items such as commissions, bonus and equity.

While my background is in sales and marketing, I know engineers, product managers and content/editors who have worked these compensation things out with their manager (it helps to pick an awesome hiring manager!).

If your current employer doesn't offer these options for pay, you might consider finding an employer that does. If you limit your pay to just salary, you will have limited increases to your compensation.

Body & Mind

Planting the 5 S.E.E.D.S™ of Weight Loss: How I Accidentally Lost 30 lbs

I lost about 30 pounds, going from 203 lbs to 171 lbs between the ages of 39 and 40. What's weird is that I wasn't trying to lose weight. It just came off steadily, most of it in six months.

So, what happened? Well, I retraced my steps and there are five items that stand out. I like acronyms, so I came up with "S.E.E.D.S" to outline the five steps (in no particular order):

S= Sleep

I watched an episode on *60 Minutes* that showed the effects of sleep deprivation on weight. One normal looking guy (my age and weight) was put in a lab and woken up periodically by alarms, creating an inconsistent sleep schedule and less sleep than normal.

The effect was he suddenly started eating twice as much food. They showed him eating an entire pizza the following day to compensate (in other words, he felt tired and food represented energy to him).

While the food certainly provided some short-term energy for him, it also added plenty more calories to his body. Seven to eight hours of sleep is widely accepted as healthy (I personally sleep an average of 7 ½).

Sleep serves us best when it is as calm and deep as possible and one way to achieve this in not to consume caffeine late in the day. A nutritionist told me that caffeine has a six-hour half-life.

That means if you drink tea or coffee at 3 p.m. and it contains 50 milligrams of caffeine, 25 milligram of caffeine will still be in your body at 9 p.m. and 12.5 milligrams will be in your body at 3 a.m. Caffeine will affect the quality of your deep sleep (while you may still fall asleep, you'll wake up groggier from the effects of the caffeine).

I now try to have my last caffeinated beverage at noon each day (except on special occasions like vacations or New Years Eve).

E = Eating

I met a nutritionist at a Japanese teahouse who taught me a visual to help with balanced eating. She drew a circle on my place mat representing a giant plate. She drew a line in the middle of it and said that half my plate should be vegetable. Then she drew a line through one of the halves so that there were two quarters and said one of those quarters should be protein (any kind you want) and the other quarter should be some sort of grain.

She also said that most people need around 1,200 to 2,500 calories per day (depending on your size, gender, how active you are) and you should spread that out over four to five meals (exceptions are if you are an active athlete or training for an event such as a marathon or triathlon, then you may need many more calories).

I have since adopted those proportions for most of my meals. The key is to make sure you have an abundance of veggies and protein around. Other eating tips I discovered during this process:

- **Read ingredients**: Read ingredients and keep a special eye on calories. Try to keep your calorie intake to 500 calories or fewer per meal.

- **Watch for sugar versus fat in snacks:** A good rule is to pick the lowest sugar snack option as sugar equates to calories. Fat is actually less important to weight loss. If you eat processed snacks, try ones that have 10 grams of sugar or fewer per serving. This is hard to find but one of my favorite low-sugar snacks is Cliff Z Bars. Beware of most energy bars as they often contain 20 to 30 grams of sugar per serving.

- **Dark chocolate rules:** If you like chocolate, I encourage you to pick as high percentage of cocoa as you can tolerate, as there is exponentially less sugar the darker the chocolate. I eat 82 percent dark chocolate and am able to have 1/3 of a large dark chocolate bar each night and its only about 70 calories. You will find triple that amount of calories in a Hershey bar or Reese's peanut butter cup. So you can eat three times as much of my dark chocolate bar than a Hershey bar (or less) and lose some weight!

- **Many meals/snacks:** When I shifted from the traditional three meals a day to four or five meals a day my weight started coming off. The key is to make each meal/snack moderate in calories.

- **Bread:** A typical slice of bread has 100 calories in it and a bagel has about 160, regardless of whether it's white, whole wheat or rye. I love bread but what I now do is eat mostly non-white (the reason is that non-white has more nutrients and fills you up faster (so you don't need as much). Another trick I use is that I try to eat bread only when its' fresh or when its' in a favorite sandwich of mine (I like BLTs!). I also try not to eat bread in a meal if I'm already having a starch such as rice or pasta.

- **Fruit:** A modest amount of fruit (or juices) any time is great. Fruit alone is good for you but beware of too much juice and smoothies! For instance, you could have the Orange Dream Machine smoothie at Jamba Juice and that's 750 calories (the equivalent of over one meal worth of calories). The largest size of Peanut Butter M'ood at Jamba Juice contains over 1,000 calories, which is two meals worth of calories for my daily diet! Too many calories at once!

E = Exercise

I had previously exercised four or five times a week and I stepped that up to daily. Some of my approaches to keeping this up are:

- **Break a sweat everyday:** I try to do something to break a sweat at least once a day (a good sex life is the easiest way)!

- **Drive less**: I try to walk or bike (instead of driving) to my destinations as much as possible. Not only does it feel better, but it helps the environment!

- **Enjoy it**: I focus my exercise on something I enjoy. I switched from treadmill jogging because it was boring for me to basketball playing, yoga, and hiking.

- **Make it a habit**: I find it's easier to exercise when I've made a habit out of it, same time of day every day!

- **Early rising:** I find that it's easier to exercise early in the day. If I wait until later in the day I find more excuses and distractions.

D = Drinking (as in less alcohol)

I cut my drinking by one third from and average of three drinks a day to two drinks a day. Doesn't sound like much but beer, wine and cocktails have about 100 to 150 calories in them.

Calories are similar to weight, so just think that one less beer or cocktail a day equates to 5 percent (100/2,000) of my daily calorie intake. Since I was 203 lbs at my peak that was 10 lbs of weight loss right there.

S = Spirituality

The fifth thing I changed during my weight loss was adding a form of spirituality: yoga. I can't explain any scientific reason why yoga helped me with weight loss, but my hunch is that it was the icing on the cake (pardon the pun) to my four other tips: sleep, eating, exercise and drinking. The main benefits I get from yoga are to let off stress and be more balanced. Since I take a Vinyasa Flow class in 75-degree temperature, I break a sweat every time so I am also getting the "E" of exercise!

How To Be An Early Riser

The smartest move I've made in years was when I began waking up early. My days became more full and fun.

Here are tips on how to be an early riser:

Get Control of Your Alarm Clock

You'll need to use an alarm clock at first (though you won't need it two weeks from now!).

What time should you pick? Be gentle with yourself at first — start with just a half-hour earlier than you're currently waking up.

I recommend you set your alarm to an unusually exact time (I picked 5:57 am)…it's been proven that you will be more responsive to unusual times (rather than on-the-hour or half-hour times (e.g. 6:00 am or 6:30 am) (see The Daily Huddle (page 138) about starting meetings at odd times).

And try to pick something soothing to wake up to (soft music or a soft voice is fine). If you're really new-agey then use one of those alarm clocks that has ocean sounds (they also have alarm clock lamps that slowly add light!).

When the alarm goes off, wake up (don't hit the snooze button!). Trust me: just get your butt out of bed.

Do something affirmative when you wake up. For instance, when I wake up, I put each foot on the floor and say "Thank" (left foot) "You" (right foot) — that starts me off on a positive note.

I promise you that within 5 minutes of waking up you will not feel like going back to bed.

Make Your First Activity Warm and Passionate

You should want to wake up earlier to do something you love...so make sure you do!

The first thing I do when I wake up is to have a hot cup of water with fresh lemon juice squeezed into it and some local honey!

Next, I have a routine for my first activity. I start with my "Hour of Power;" that consists of me sitting in a comfortable chair on the East side of my apartment (where the sun is rising) and writing down a few creative things that I'd like to do for the next hour.

Then I do them! Sometimes it's reading a book, other times it's playing guitar and sometimes it's writing (like this article).

I then go work out for an hour (basketball or yoga).

Whatever you do, try to avoid reactive tasks such as reading emails or paying the bills. Go with proactive/creative stuff.

Beware Caffeine's Six-Hour Half-Life

If you consume caffeine (I do), you're going to need to consume your last sip a bit earlier (I recommend 1pm at the latest).

The reason is that caffeine has what's called a 6-hour half-life, meaning that if you have a cup of coffee (average of 50 milligrams of caffeine) at 3pm, then you will still have 25 milligrams of coffee at 9pm — it's the equivalent of you drinking a half-cup of coffee at 9pm at night!

Some of you might say: "I drink caffeine late in the day and still get my eight hours of shut-eye." I believe you. But your 8 hours probably isn't very restful sleep...you may wake up groggy (that's because you didn't get enough deep sleep).

For those of you hooked on caffeine, just start to wean yourself off of the afternoon habit by switching to decaf (still has some caffeine) or a white tea (has a little caffeine in it) or an herbal tea (no caffeine).

I drink one cup of a black or green tea at about 9:30am and then I have a decaffeinated latte (fancy, I know) at about 12noon.

With less caffeine in you at night, you'll sleep more restfully, and it will be easier for you to wake up early every day!

When to Go To Sleep: Have a Book You Love

As you get into this process of waking up early, you'll begin to naturally get tired earlier at night. This may take about a week.

But what time should you go to sleep? Steve Pavlina recommends simply going to sleep when you're tired in his terrific 'How to Become an Early Riser' article.

What I do is get into bed 8 to 8 ½ hours before my desired wake up time (e.g. around 9:30pm to wake up at 5:57 pm).

I then start reading a book until I'm sleepy.

It's important to pick a book you love so that you'll look forward to going to bed! I fall asleep within 30 minutes (that's how I get my 7 1/2 to 8 hours sleep). .

Commit to a Week

Practice your new waking up early for at least seven days…by that time, you will start getting used to it.

You'll naturally wake up earlier (you won't even need an alarm clock within about three weeks) and fall asleep earlier too.

You'll love waking up earlier so much that you'll test out waking up earlier and earlier until you find the ideal time.

As the saying goes, the early bird really does get the worm.

While I'm a big fan of being an early riser, please remember about the importance of sleep as a form of renewal.

Postscript: *After first writing my How To Be An Early Riser article, I began jotting down examples of other early risers — especially famous early risers. I thought I'd share those with you:*

Famous Early Risers:

- Leo Babauta (Blog Writer) — 4:30 am
- Mary Higgins Clark (Writer) — Often began writing 5 am.
- Winston Churchill — He would wake up at 7:30 am and work from bed until 11:00 am.
- Benjamin Franklin -- Famous for his quote: "Early to bed and early to rise makes a man healthy, wealthy and wise."
- Sylvia Plath (Writer) — Often began writing at 5am.

How To Drink Alcohol More Moderately

My father had a problem drinking -- he drank too much.

I have that tendency as well. I came up with a little program that helped me gain control.

First off, I started to keep a drinking diary of how much I drank each day and any notes related to it. For example, "two glasses of wine and a shot of tequila" is the quantity and then the note might be where and when I had the drinks, "Dinner with Ted, Kelly and Jane from 8 pm to 10 pm. "

I kept doing this in my journal for about a week. How much is ok to drink? I encourage you to do your own studies but a general rule of thumb (health wise) is on average one to two drinks per day is ok for a woman and two to three per day is ok for a man (one drink being about five ounces of beer, wine or a mixed cocktail).

Binge drinking (six or seven drinks over an hour or two) is generally a bad idea. When I drink more than two drinks in a row, I try to stick to a limit of one drink per hour (for that day) as it typically takes one hour for alcohol to leave your system. I remember that from driver's education.

Some tips to keep drinking within control:

1. **Try drinking one glass of water for every alcoholic drink you consume.** This is a good idea for hydration and also slows your pace of drinking alcohol.

2. **Reduce your "drinking window."** If you're a night drinker, for instance, you may notice that you're drinking from 7 pm, when you come home from work, until 10 pm. Try to narrow that window to two hours at first. When I started going to sleep earlier (10 pm versus 11 pm) I noticed that I drank less because my drinking window shrank.

3. **Drink only with food.** If you are a wine drinker like I am, try drinking wine only when you are eating and not before or after. I have a glass of wine with my dinner and then another glass of wine with some chocolate for dessert.

4. **Drink tea.** Instead of making your first drink alcohol, try making it a cup of decaffeinated tea and then also try having a cup of decaf tea in place of the last alcoholic drink you were planning on consuming. It's hard to believe but you may find that you actually enjoy the tea more than whatever you were drinking. You can also substitute water for tea.

5. **Talk about it with close friends.** There is nothing wrong with talking with friends about the fact that you're trying to drink less alcohol. It may seem a bit weird, but if they are truly your friends they won't judge you and will instead support you.

A Couple Of Tips On Depression

I am by no means an expert on depression but I have a couple of experiences that may be helpful. During Thanksgiving dinner around the time I was in junior high school, my dad walked up to the dinner table (where my two sisters and I were seated while my mom was in the kitchen) and declared:

> "I have just spent the last seven months in a type of depression, a melancholy, and I'm now out of it and doing ok. One thing that really helped me get though this challenge was a book called *Darkness Visible* by William (Bill) Styron. If you or anyone you know ever suffers from a challenge with depression, I recommend you utilized this book."

He then handed us each a copy. Well, years later when I was around 27 years old, I went through my own period of despair. Two close friends had killed themselves and my parents were separating. I felt a melancholy for weeks, then months and I just couldn't get out of it.

Life seemed hopeless and nothing I did could shake the feeling. Suicide was a topic I thought about often as my two friends had chosen that path. Then, I remembered my dad's *Darkness Visible* book recommendation (I still had it!), and read it in one sitting during a retreat at Orr Hot Spring in Ukiah, CA (a great place to reflect!).

What resonated with me so much from the book was its first-hand account of author Bill Styron experiencing depression. It was the first glimpse of hope I had felt in months.

Reading it felt like meeting someone who was in exactly the same pickle as me. It marked the beginning of the end of my melancholy.

I now recommend it to anyone who is experiencing any level of depression. I believe it can save you or your loved one's life.

When It Gets Stressful

4 Simple Tips To Help Make
Tough "50-50" Decisions

I have four decision-making approaches I use on a regular basis.

These are techniques to use when there's a real close call ("50-50" so to speak) to make; they are often the most important decisions you'll make.

My nephew Miles drew this awesome image of a person having a tough time making a decision. I think it might be a combination of me and my dad!

1) Decide Based On The Tougher Choice

If it's a REALLY tough decision on whether to take action or not take action, it is often the tougher decision that turns out to be the right one. For instance, if I have been dwelling about letting go of an employee who is under-performing, I have always found that the right move was to let them go.

The reason I don't immediately make that decision is because it's the tougher one to make and so I drag my feet a bit.

Or, when I was single, I was often given the choice of going out to a social event versus staying home for a quiet evening: staying home was the easier route to take but it wasn't going to find me a girlfriend (an important goal at the time!). The tougher choice (showering, putting on some nice duds and traveling to the social event) was really the right call.

2) Decide To Take "The Road Less Travelled"

I think we can all benefit from Robert Frost's advice for life in general: "I took the road less travelled by, and that has made all the difference."

3) The "Win-Win Exercise Gets You The Best Of Both Worlds

I wrote about the Win-Win Exercise on page 63 – this is best used when there are enough variables at play in a decision that it's worth jotting them down into pros and cons. It's not a simple pros and cons exercise: go check it out as it's got a surprise twist that enables you to get the best of both worlds in the decision you make.

4) If None Of The Above Decision-Making Tips Work... Then Do This

If you have a decision about two actions to take, and a spirited debate can be made for either side, Eugene Kleiner, a venture capitalist, had a great rule of thumb: "Either action you choose is likely going to be ok (hint: so don't beat yourself up over which action to take)." So, in that case, basically, flip a coin!

Feeling Disorganized:
Do The Hardest Thing First

I was 25 years old and flying from New York to San Francisco when I sat next to Stephanie Winston, author of a book called "Getting Organized". I wasn't much of a reader then, so I said brashly:

"You know, I'm sure your book is quite good, but knowing myself I'll never read it. If you had to give me just one tip on getting organized what would it be?"

Her single tip was this. When you are facing a bunch of things to do, it's usually a good idea to do the hardest thing first and the easiest thing last. Specifically, she said that most people's productivity is higher in the beginning of the day and they are less productive at the end of the day.

A mistake many folks make is that they put off the hard thing to do until later in the day and unfortunately they are running out of gas at that point and the task becomes all the more stressful (and usually doesn't get done!).

Law Of Variables: Change As Few Of These As Possible At The Same Time

When making a change (or "variable") in my life, I find that I should make as few as possible and the ideal number of variables at a time is one. For example, a friend of mine, Priscilla, met a guy who proposed to her (no his name wasn't Elvis): and then around the same time asked her to move into a new house that they would buy together....and the purchase of the home would be right around the time of the wedding.

Most people have a hard time focusing on one major event (project, challenge) at a time. Well, getting married and moving is what I consider two pretty major projects in life.

Priscilla was feeling super stressed about buying a new home AND getting married. I advised her to put some time between her two big events. Her fiancé caught wind of this and it cost me an invitation to their wedding (no kidding). But I believed that strongly in it.

Try to support your loved ones who might face multiple variables at the same time. Take my ex-girlfriend for instance. She moved with me from New York to San Francisco and changed her home, her job and her group of friends at the same time. This was very tough on her.

You might ask, isn't that just the way it goes when you move across the country? Well, it doesn't have to be. When I moved from New York to San Francisco I kept my same job and luckily I had a close friend living in SF. So I really had only one major variable (my home) change.

And it was a much easier transition for me. Here are examples of the major variables in life that I'm talking about, try to change no more than one or two at a time when possible:

- Romantic relationships
- Moving homes
- Losing a job
- Changing jobs
- Changing schools
- Death of a loved one
- Surgery or any health issue
- Friendship

If You're Feeling Stressed By Too Many Tasks

I heard about a great exercise from my friend Eben. On the left-hand half of a page, list out all the things that are worrying you (these are typically things that need to be done). Leave room to the right of the things you wrote down and then rank them on a scale of 1 to 10, where 10 is the thing you're worrying about the most.

Then write down next to the things that are worrying you the most logical next action step you will take to address that worry. Even if you do nothing else at this point, you should feel less stressed.

Then the real kicker is to do the action steps for the 10's, followed by the 9's. Don't worry about the lower ranked items of 8 and below because the 9's and 10's are typically where it's at and by focusing on them you will feel better about everything else.

If you can get that far, your stress on those times will dissipate, I promise! I actually used this approach, writing out a list every day with rankings of how much I'm worried about them, as my daily to-do list for a while!

3 Stages Of Dealing With A Problem: Negative, Neutral And Positive

Life is full of problems and it always will be. So if you accept that it's how you deal with them that counts! When a problem arrives, I look at three stages of being in it and getting out of it. For example, I recently hurt my ankle and that presented a problem with my playing basketball. My sports therapist said that I wouldn't be able to run on the basketball court for two to three months.

Here are the three stages:

1) **Be Negative:** I could have been bummed out and simply not deal with playing basketball for a few months. *That sucks.*

2) **Neutralize:** I could focus on replacing basketball with some low-impact activity I enjoy less like swimming or biking. *That's the least I could do.*

3) **Be Positive:** I could focus on improving my basketball game utilizing low-impact training such as watching YouTube basketball videos, and practicing my ball handling and shooting.

I chose option 3, to be positive, and an amazing thing happened. Michael Jordan showed me (in a YouTube video) a new one-on-one move, my ball handling became much better and I tested out jumping off of my right foot. Before, I had mostly jumped off my now-injured left foot, jumping off my right foot allowed me some new moves.

So my ankle injury started off as a negative event but has now proven positive! I believe that every negative in life can become a positive! In fact, turning negativity into positivity may be one of the true secrets to happiness (though I still miss layups on a regular basis!).

Business Basics

3 Simple Steps To Run An Effective Meeting: The GAP Approach

$\mathbf{I}$ get asked about how to run effective meetings all the time. As I wrote about on page 139 on the Daily Huddle, how you run meetings has a material effect on your business. I believe that the difference between a dull meeting and an amazing meeting is how you organize it.

I learned about one meeting agenda format used by a consultant to a Johnson & Johnson subsidiary and I think it works just great. It's called G.A.P and it stands for Goal, Agenda and Preparation. I believe every meeting should have all three!

Goal

The goal, or purpose, of the meeting needs to be stated upfront. A good way to remember what goes into a goal (for meetings or anything else) is that it should be a SMART Goal as in:

S = The goal should be **S**pecific

M = The goal should be **M**easureable

A = The goal should be **A**chievable

R = The goal should be **R**elevant

T = The goal should be **T**imely (it should be reachable by the time the meeting ends)

That gets you off to the right start to a SMART meeting!

Agenda

When you hold a meeting, you need to have an agenda...even if the agenda is to have no agenda. Huh? What I'm saying is that you as the meeting organizer need to state how the attendees are going to use the time at the meeting. The agenda could be something as simple as:

1.   Description of problem you face (10 minutes)

2.   Input from each team member (10 minutes)

3.   Recommendation on next steps (10 minutes)

Or, if you're not going to have something so structured, then state that the agenda is:

•   Open Discussion (30 minutes)

Preparation

A key to most meetings is preparation (by you the meeting organizer and by the attendees). So, if you call a meeting, tell the attendees what they need to do to prepare.

When they join the meeting, should they have already reviewed a spread sheet that you sent out? Do they need to have collected information from someone inside or outside the company? Tell them how to prepare...if there's no advanced preparation then I like to just say: "No Preparation...Just Bring Your Brain."

If you use online calendars to schedule meetings, you should put the entire Goal, Agenda and Preparation (GAP) within your calendar invitation. Follow GAP and you'll have better meetings.

6 Tips On Striking Business Partnerships

You likely need partnerships to grow your business. Here are some tips I've used to close partnerships with such companies as Disney, Microsoft, Sprint, Sony Music and NBC.

1. **What's Your Endgame** — As Stephen Covey says in The 7 Habits of Highly Effective People, start with the end in mind. Imagine the press release you would like to announce your partnership; be as specific as possible.

2. **Establish the "What" before the "How"** — Make sure to be clear with yourself and partner on "what" it is you're both trying to do before you dive into the how. An example of a "what": you may want traffic from your partner's Web site to your own; and they may want you to pay them to advertise on their Web site. An example of a "How" would be: Your partner will put a link for your Web site on their Web site.

3. **Those who listen the most, win** — Don't talk too much: focus on your partner's challenges.

4. **Ask a lot of questions** — As I pointed out in my article on Spin Selling, ask a lot of questions (especially about what your partner's objective is). A favorite question of mine is: "What's your biggest challenge?"

5. **Be direct & honest** — Don't beat around the bush. Be as honest and direct with your partner on what you want as possible.

6. **Determine the fit first/business model later** — Focus on getting to know each other and finding the partnership fit first,

before you get caught up in negotiating. The business terms will be much easier once you've fallen a bit in love as partners.

How To Improve Your Team By Playing One Of These Four "D.A.C.I." Roles

Know thy role!

My love Jane turned me on to a framework that she learned at Johnson & Johnson's BabyCenter…it's called DACI and it stands for: **D = Driver, A = Approver, C = Consulted and I = Informed.** The DACI model has helped me execute numerous projects more efficiently! Here's how it works:

When you are trying to get something done, ask yourself: "Who can serve in the following roles?"

Driver = This is the most important role. It's the person who drives a project from start to completion — it's their neck on the line to get this thing done! This is typically one person but you can be two "co-drivers."

For larger projects, I highly recommend that you pick a highly organized and detail-oriented person to be the driver. A less-organized person works fine as the driver on small projects involving fewer people and items to organize.

The DACI driver's responsibilities typically include:

- Calling an initial kick-off meeting to discuss the purpose of the project

- Collecting ideas & feedback on the project from those inside and outside the company

  note: those people are also known as consultants (see next page)

- Creating a detailed step-by-step plan for the project including tasks that need to get done, deadlines and how the project will be measured

- Organizing follow-up meetings to hold people accountable for their assigned tasks and measure progress

- Communicating updates on the project regularly

- Lead the completion of the project

Note: The driver doesn't have to be the smartest person on a particular topic and in fact I find that the smartest person on a particular topic often doesn't make a good driver (they make a good consultant)

Approver = The person who will approve the project (aka "the boss" or a senior manager)

Consulted = These are the experts that the driver will call upon to consult him or her. This can be the largest group and it is up to the driver to make sure to find and utilize consultants

Informed = These are the people who need to be informed about the progress of the project. They will include all the people above — the Driver, Approver and Consulted — and possibly others who want to be updated on the project but aren't actively involved.

So, next time you're trying to get something done: Try using the **DACI** approach…and get in touch with knowing thy role!

Do These 3 Things And
You'll Be A Much Better Networker

I was stunned recently when, within 15 minutes of a concert I attended, I found a potential buyer for my 94 year-old grandma's summer cottage 2,000 miles across the country.

How did I do it? This wasn't just luck — although you could argue that the tips I'm going to share are all ways to increase your luck...or serendipity as I like to call it. Either way, it was a positive thing...so I re-engineered what happened and am sharing the three tips below.

I really like these 3 networking tips because they are easy to do and remember.

Networking Tip #1: Attend Events You Enjoy (It's That Easy!)

The first thing I did was to attend an event I knew I'd enjoy. A friend had invited me to a "Tribute To Jerry Garcia" concert put on by the REX Foundation...and I'm a huge live music/Jerry Garcia fan! Why is attending an event you'll enjoy so important to networking? Because you are going to be most comfortable and amicable when you're doing something you enjoy — and you'll be surrounded by people who share your passion.

This reminds me of a dating advice tip I once learned from my friend/colleague David DeAngelo (aka Eben Pagan), the author of *Double Your Dating*. David D. would tell men that it's a lot easier meeting women while doing your favorite hobby then it is at a bar (unless your hobby is drinking...in which case you've got some additional challenges).

The same is true of networking — I was comfortable at this "Tribute to Jerry Garcia" event and feeling more conversational with a few people around me before the show began. That's when I met Denis.

Networking Recommendation: Think of a few of your favorite hobbies (e.g. sports, books, food, knitting, photography, Star Trek, etc.) and try networking during one of those.

Networking Tip #2: Ask Questions ("Break The Ice!")

If you've been reading my blog (such as my piece on How To Sell Better through Spin Selling) you've heard me talk about how important asking questions is to your success. Networking is no different: you need to ask people questions to connect with people. That's what happened with Denis and I: he was sitting at a table with a few of us and we started chatting about basic stuff like:

"Where are you from? Have you seen this band before?".

That's when Denis mentioned that he had grown up near the town of Woodstock, New York (and he had attended Woodstock the event!). My grandma has a house about an hour's drive from Woodstock. That's when this dialogue ensued:

Me: "Where exactly did you grow up?"

Denis: "The Catskills"

Me: "Where exactly in the Catskills?"

Denis: "South Fallsburg"

I nearly fell out of my chair.

Me: "My grandma's got a place in South Fallsburg."

Denis: "You don't say! Where's her house?"

Networking Tip #3: Be Organized (Thank God For my iPhone & Google Docs!)

So, now things are getting interesting. Denis and I have figured out that he grew up in the same small town as my Grandma! And my

Grandma and her South Fallsburg home have been on my mind lately as she doesn't much use it any more…I've been thinking that she might want to sell it. Denis then asks me if I know what road her house is on.

I whipped out my iPhone and pulled up a Google Doc that my family had set up about my Grandma's financial planning and I found the address of her summer cottage.

When I told Denis the street address he nearly fell out of his chair and said: "That's where I grew up — my dad still lives there…right across the street!"

Then Denis made my night when he added: "And my dad has wanted to buy that property for a long time!" The connection Denis and I experienced would not have been nearly as strong had I not had the address of my grandma's property on hand. I'm not the most organized guy in the world, but I was organized enough that night.

Networking Recommendation: Try keeping addresses, phone numbers and other key information well organized and accessible (Smart Phones are a wonderful invention as they allow you to carry a huge amount of data/information in your pocket!).

I'm also a big fan of Google Docs for keeping notes about things: it's free and searchable. I use Google Docs for notes on people I speak with and projects I work on. And because it sits in the cloud, it's usually very easy for access (whether you have a Smart Phone or not) as long as you have Web access nearby. Denis and I were able to follow up by phone the week after the concert to discuss his dad and my grandma…and I look forward to getting to know his family better.

To recap our networking tips, if you focus on:

1. Attending events you enjoy

2. Asking fellow-attendees questions

3. Organizing yourself well

…you'll become a better networker.

How To Create A Sales Pipeline

I was teaching someone on our team about how a sales pipeline works — so I thought I'd summarize my sales approach here for you (I've used this for straight up sales as well as for partner sales).

Note: I'm going to refer to the party I'm selling to as a "customer" but it could easily be a partner in the case of partnership sales.

There are any number of sales pipeline stages you can use: I'm going to use Leads, 10% Opportunities, 50% Opportunities, 90% Opportunities and Closed Won/Lost. I first adopted this methodology when I began using Salesforce.com, which mapped well to how my mind works.

Stage 1: LEADS

First you have to get leads in the door. What is a lead? A lead is a potential customer at its earliest stage. Some people call this a sales "prospect." So, what is a prospect and what's the difference between lead and prospect?

I think using either "lead" or "prospect" is fine, though in sales I tend to prefer to use lead to define my earliest stage potential customer. I then use prospect more as a verb as what I have to do to find leads (e.g. when I read about a potential customer in the newspaper or on a Web site I am "prospecting.").

For example, here are the criteria I used for qualifying sales leads (qualifying leads may be quite different based on what industry you are in):

- I have their first and last name.

- I have their company name.

- I have a quantity metric helping me to understand that they have enough value to merit me working for them (examples of a quantity metric might include the number of employees they have, the amount of revenue they generate or their Web site's traffic ranking).

- I have a quality metric helping me understand if they are the type of lead I'm looking for (examples include: the vertical market they are in or the title of the individual)

Prospecting sales leads is a full-time job. There are two main types of leads:

1) Inbound Leads

To generate inbound leads, you can simply run advertisements (leaving your phone number, email or Web site information) or it may be as simple as you have a Web site with a "Contact Us" link that leads to a sales lead form (which of course would ask for the type of information (such as their size, type of business, etc.) that helps you define whether someone is a good lead.

2) Outbound Leads

Outbound lead generation consists primarily of having an outbound marketing program or outbound sales (such as outbound telesales). The point is that generating outbound leads consists of proactively making a day-to-day effort to find leads.

The next stage after qualifying a lead is turning it into what I call an "opportunity." I have three stages of opportunities: 10%, 50% and 90% — let me explain each.

Stage 2: OPPORTUNITY (10%) ("We have connected with the right people at the right business")

I define a 10% Opportunity as having the following qualifications:

- I have made contact with them.

- I have confirmed that the quantity is there for my type of customer (for example, they have a top 1,000 Web site if I'm looking to sell to the largest Web sites in the world).

- I have confirmed a quality metric such as they are in a vertical market that has worked for me in the past or another example is that the person I'm talking to is the proper decision-maker for closing a deal with me).

- Finally, and this sounds obvious, but I define a 10% opportunity as one that has a 1 in 10 chance of closing — duh!

Stage 3: OPPORTUNITY (50%) ("We're in the ballpark on this deal")

I define a 50% opportunity as having the following qualifications:

- The details of the product or partnership have been discussed and it's agreed it's a good fit for both sides.

- The pricing of the deal is in the ballpark (within 20%).

- The rough timing of the close of the deal has been discussed.

Stage 4: OPPORTUNITY (90%) ("Negotiations are complete")

I define a 90% Opportunity as meeting the following criteria:

- Agreement on pricing.

- Agreement on product specs.

- Agreement on closing date.

- Agreement on delivery date of product.

- Contract has been reviewed (just not signed yet).

Stage 5: Closed Won (or Lost) (100%)

Finally, when you close a deal you have two scenarios:

1) You closed the deal meaning you won it. That means that you have the contract in hand and you're off to the races!

2) You closed the deal because you lost it. This is ok. Think about the old story of the vacuum cleaner salesman who sold vacuums for $100 but had to knock on 50 doors to get a sale. Well, each "Closed Lost" deal of his was worth $2, right!?

Salesforce Automation

Finally, there are plenty of customer relationship manager software programs (aka CRM software) available to help you with the stages above. Most include the basics of:

- Sales pipeline management.

- Sales pipeline templates.

- Sales pipeline reports.

I happen to use Salesforce.com and I'm quite happy with it...but there's plenty of other good sales software out there. And don't forget to check out my favorite book on Selling — read my article on it here: SPIN Selling.

The Seven Unusual Fundraising Lessons I Learned While Raising $1 Million +

I've raised money twice: $1 million for ExpressDoctors (a flop) and $350,000 for Mojam (which got sold!).

I'm by no means a pro — you'll find many others with more experience — but I don't see too many of them writing about how they did it...so I will.

I'm leaving out the "Fundraising 101" type tips such as: Define the uses of the money you need; investing takes longer than you think; have a good business plan, have a name-brand/or trustworthy bank and law firm to process paperwork, etc. — you can find those tips anywhere.

My seven tips on how to raise money are, hopefully, a bit outside the box.

1) Create An Investor Pipeline

Name	Potential Investment	Probability	Potential Net Yield	Source
Fred Flinstone	$100,000	75%	$75,000	He's my best friend
Your father in law	$75,000	50%	$37,500	Went to school with my Dad
Mark Zuckerberg	$500,000	6%	$30,000	Grew up near me
Steve Jobs	$1,000,000	2%	$20,000	He owes me a favor (I wrote about his startup when it was struggling)
Rupert Murdoch	$500,000	4%	$20,000	Grandson
Richard Branson	$500,000	4%	$20,000	We always have fun on the island.
Bill Gates	$1,000,000	2%	$20,000	I've interviewed him a few times...maybe he remembers
Barney Rubble	$400,000	4%	$16,000	Fred F.
George Jetson	$300,000	2%	$6,000	A future thinker
Barack Obama	$200,000	2%	$4,000	White House custodian
Charlie Sheen	$100,000	2%	$2,000	Ted Koppel
Totals	$4,675,000		$250,500	

Crafting an investor pipeline is an easy and effective way to help raise money.

The reason you need to create a pipeline is that fundraising is simply a sales/numbers game (just like I explained on page 104 on How To Create A Sales Pipeline) — you're going to approach X # of people who will pay you $Y amount of money and some will turn you down and some will actually invest (if you work hard!).

The key with the pipeline is to make your best guess as to how much they might invest and what the probability is that you could close them on that investment — you multiply those together and you get your "Potential Net Yield."

Why?

The Potential Net Yield will help you rank which investor to focus on (even though Fred Flintstone (in the pipeline above) doesn't have as much money to invest ($100K) as Steve Jobs ($1 Million), Fred might be someone to focus on first because he's your best friend and the probability is so high that you'll get him to invest, that's a better use of your time.

The Potential Net Yield is also important in determining how many investors you should approach. In the pipeline example above, if you approached all 12 of the investor prospects, you'd have a crack at raising $250,500 (the total Potential Net Yield). If you need to raise $1 million, you better add a lot more prospects (or increase your probability for each of your current prospects).

2) It Takes The Same Amount Of Time To Get A $100,000 Check As It Does A $1,000 Check

This old cliché from business: "It takes as long to do a small deal as it does a big deal," is mostly true. I don't mean that it's just as easy to get your father-in-law to give you $100,000 as it is for him to hand you $1,000 — what I mean is that if you have two investors and their profile is this:

- Fred Flintstone with a net worth of $500,000; and

- Your grandfather with a net worth of $5 million (10X the net worth of Fred Flintstone!)

...then — all other things equal — getting a check from Fred for $10,000 is going to be just as hard as getting a check from your grandfather for $100,000 *(hint: focus more on your grandpa!)*.

Case in point: A friend of mine — who prides himself on being democratic/socialist — wanted to raise $250,000 from "friends and family" and he was dead-set on trying to get 10 of them to each invest exactly $25,000 apiece and in return they'd each get 1% of the company.

I warned him against this — "There is no reason you have to treat each of your investors exactly the same!" One of his friends might be able to afford $100,000 and another friend might only be able to afford $10,000 — so treat them each with the uniqueness they deserve. He convinced a couple of people to put in $25K but failed to raise the money he needed.

3) "Social Proof" — The First Investor Is Key

Raising money at every stage is hard — but the first check you get from someone is WAY harder than all subsequent checks. This is Psychology 101 — many call it "Social Proof." Few people want to be the first — but many folks don't mind being second or third.

Use this to your advantage — try to focus your first talks with people who have a high probability of backing you. It will also boost your confidence immensely.

I had the good fortune of having the CEO of my ex-employer (Michael Leeds) offer to be the first investor in my Mojam startup (for which I am eternally grateful). The second and third investors were MUCH easier — I'd even go so far as to suggest that the 2nd and 3rd investors were 10X easier than the first investor.

4) Leverage As Many "Unfair Advantages" As You Have

Investors are like anyone else — they are typically motivated by their self-interests. The easiest example is money (though many will be motivated by changing the world/giving back, etc.). Regardless of which motivation they have, they will want to hear what your unfair advantages are. Examples of unfair advantages are:

- Unique access to an audience

- Clients lined up who have agreed to pay you

- Exclusive content

- Technology that's beyond anyone else

- A key co-founder with lots of experience

5) Focus On The Person, Not The Firm

If you're raising money from a firm (e.g. venture capital, private equity), don't lose sight of the fact that there is one human being there who needs to champion you. Your "selling" of this individual is your way of getting the entire firm on-board. Start with the individual, not the entire firm.

6) Who Is In "The Syndicate"?

The leading angel investors in Silicon Valley are parts of "syndicates" — they invest with others they know. "Super-Angel" investor Ron Conway is said to prefer to invest only once certain other investors (his "syndicate") have committed. So, if you happen to hear that about one of your investor prospects, you obviously want to focus on the other members of the Syndicate.

7) Investor Relationships Are Best Measured In Years (Not Weeks Or Months)

The longer you have known your potential investor, the easier it will be to raise money from them (assuming you've shown yourself to be of high integrity). So, if you're even thinking about raising money, start focusing on building trusting relationships with your prospects...that's easier to do now than it is when you're asking them for a check. I wouldn't invest in anyone I haven't known for a couple of years...unless they were endorsed by my "syndicate."

Communication

7 Tips For Writing Like Warren Buffett

I'm willing to bet you that half of Warren Buffet's success is due to his effective communication. Most of his other half is his sustained focus (i.e. his singular focus on creating wealth over 60 years!). If you don't believe me, you should read his annual reports or watch video of him on CNBC and YouTube.

Some people, including me, refer to his communication style as "Plain English."

Here are seven tips for using the plain English style of writing used by Buffett, Mark Twain and others:

#1: Focus On Personal Pronouns

Focus on the first-person plural (we, us, our/ours) and second person singular (you and yours). The purpose is it's more direct, more conversational and avoids the he/she dilemma.

For example:

(Before/Poor) — "This article will enlighten readers and contribute to people's success."

Versus:

(After/Better)- "I will enlighten you in this article and contribute to your success."

#2: No Weak Verbs!

Steer clear of verbs such as "to be" and "to have." They are weak! Take the following sentence for example:

(Before/Poor) — "We will make a distribution of cash to every person in the company if our business is ever sold."

versus

(After/Better) — "We will distribute cash to everyone in our company if we are sold"

Hint: nouns that usually end in "ion" can be replaced with a more powerful verb (in that case, "Will distribute" replaced "will make a distribution").

#3: Write in the Positive

Use "unable" instead of "not able" and "exclude" instead of "not include," etc. — This is shorter and more clear.

#4: Active Voice (Instead of Passive Voice)

Try to use active (as opposed to passive) voice and go in order of subject, verb and object.

For example:

(Before/Poor) — "The product is bought by the customer"

(After/Better) — "The customer buys the product."

#5: Avoid Superfluous Words

Try to avoid words that don't add much value such as "in order to" (use "to") and "Despite the fact that" (use "Although"). Why? Readers understand sentences in the active voice more quickly and easily because it follows how we think and process information

#6: Communicating To A Group (With One In Mind)

When communicating, you should know your audience…that's basic, but if you're communicating to a number of people try to write with a certain person in mind. For example, in this article I try to envision writing to Lakshmi, a department head of a medium-sized business I know.

When I'm writing about something technical, I write with my Mom in mind.

#7: Avoid Contract Language

Steer clear of "contract-type" language with definitions — this is the opposite of Plain English. The best book on the subject of Plain English is How to write, speak and think more effectively by Rudolf Flesch. And then there are Warren Buffett's famous annual reports.

Plain English, please!

Trick To Determine If Someone Is A Bull Shitter

There are times when it's useful to know if someone is putting you on (i.e. if they are a bull shitter).

When I'm getting to know someone new, I will ask them a question about a topic for which I am knowledgeable just to hear their answer and determine if they are bull shitting.

For instance, if they say they are a Google expert, I'll ask them,

"What are a few basic tips about how to get your Web site to show up in the top spots on Google?"

You will notice that wise people will admit that they don't know much about that topic (unless they do!). And the bull shitters will continue to sling their bull!

This is a great interview technique!

4 Steps To Crafting An Effective Email

If you're like me, you craft email messages just about every day. I'm amazed at how many poorly written emails I see on a regular basis (and some I don't see clearly because they're confusing).

Here are some basic rules I try to use for every message: (I'm using the example of a hypothetical partnership with Google as the topic at hand):

1) Clear Subject Line

The purpose of the subject line is to be clear about the subject (duh) and to get the recipient to open it (if relevant to them).

Examples using the hypothetical Google partnership topic:

"Google Partnership" (Good)

"Google Partnership Closed: Next Steps" (Better)

"Google Partnership: Your Input Needed" (Best)

2) The "Door Opener"

The opening sentence or two of the actual message should be crystal clear about what you want from the recipient(s).

Examples:

"I would like your thoughts on section five of the attached contract for our Google Partnership."

" We closed the Google partnership today — way to go, team!"

"I just got off the phone with Larry and Sergey about our deal; here are our next steps."

3) The "Meat" of the Message

The next part of your message should include any important data or other information necessary for the recipient to be aware of.

Examples:

"Attached is the language in Section five. Are you comfortable with payment terms described in it?"

"Now that the Google partnership is closed, would you please set up the kick-off call with Sergey and Larry to get things going!?"

4) The Closer

You should close with what action you'd like the recipient to take and any timing if applicable.

Examples:

"I'd appreciate your input by Friday as I have a Monday morning meeting with Google."

"Thank you for your work on closing the Google deal. Please put it in your calendar for July 15th to review its performance."

"Please make sure to alert our finance team to expect the Google wire transfer by Monday at 11 a.m."

If you follow these four steps for your email communication, you'll speed things along and face fewer unpleasant surprises.

I Don't Know – Say It!

I recently learned the power of saying "I don't know".

I once thought that I always had to have an answer. Well, the fact is that I sometimes just don't know an answer to something…so now I say:

"I don't know."

I find when people hear my "I don't know" response they are usually quite appreciative and respectful. A calm feeling often emerges.

In fact, very often, it gives them an opportunity to ask their question differently (or to ask someone else who probably has a better answer).

And strangely, saying "I don't know" feels good.

How To Write Better Headlines In 10 Easy Tips

The "Dean Of Copywriters" John Caples famously said that an effective marketing piece/ad can have 19.5 times the success of a poorly written ad.

And the most important aspect of advertising is the headline. In fact, five times as many people read headlines as read the body copy of an ad, according to ad guru David Ogilvy.

The headline of this ad is considered one of the most effective in the history of advertising due to its appeal to self-interest and curiosity.

Maybe you're not directly in marketing/advertising, so should you care? Big time! If you do any of the following you will benefit from improving your headline writing skills:

- Write emails (the subject line is your headline)

- Name things (whether your product or your business or, in some cases, your child!)

- Write blog postings

- Write a description of yourself on your resume or LinkedIn profile

I'm by no means a copywriting expert, but I hang out with some and I've studied some of the greats (David Oglivy, Al Ries, Jack Trout, John Caples).

So I am going to share 10 awesome headline-writing tips I've learned along the way.

10 Tips On How To Write Effective Headline

1) Write The Headline First

The purpose of the headline is to get the reader to keep on reading the body/copy of your messaging. So don't wait until the end of writing your copy or article to come up with the headline. Think a bunch about it first.

When I write my articles (such as for this blog), I first pick a topic I'm interested/or know a bit about (e.g. "Headline Writing") and then I spend a little time (in this case 10 minutes) working on the headline. Then I write the article.

2) Always State A Clear Benefit For The Reader

Almost all great headlines have a clear benefit to the reader. Everyone has self-interests and you must focus on that in your headline in order to get the person to continue reading.

I use the Google AdWords Keyword tool to research the topic I'm interested in writing. The Keyword Tool shows how many people are searching certain topics and it really helps me get in their shoes and to appeal to their potential benefit/self-interest.

For example, when I searched the keyword tool for "writing headlines" I found that 260 people per month search the term "How To Write A Headline" – so I used that as the main "benefit" in my headline above.

I added in a further benefit (increasing response rates by 19.5X) as well as "10 Easy Tips" (see tip #5 on page 125) so that it's crystal clear who this article is for: anyone who wants to get some easy tips on how to write better headlines and increase their sales!

3) Pique Their Curiosity

People are curious by nature, and you can add that to the benefit to create some killer headlines. An example of a headline with curiosity would be: "The 7 Home Safety Tips The FBI Doesn't Want You To Know About."

4) News Sells

Ogilvy says headlines with news perform 22% better than those without news. Some tips on working news into your headlines (thanks to John Caples) are:

- Begin with the word "Introducing" or "Announcing" (e.g. "Introducing The New Best-Selling Book On Headline Writing!")

- Begin with the word "New" or "Now" (e.g. "New Floss Has Toothpaste Built In So You Don't Need To Brush").

123

- Put a date into your headline: "Coming September 7th, The Hottest TV Show The Critics Are Raving About"

5) Emphasize Short Cuts

Caples also points out how people love shortcuts — so you can work what he calls "Quick & Easy Ways" of doing things into your headline. If you look at some of my recent headlines, for example, you'll find that I use "Quick & Easy" on a regular basis:

"5 Easy Ways To Increase Serendipity"

"4 Simple Tips To Help You Make ("50-50") Tough Decisions"

"6 Easy Tools To Name Stuff On The Web"

6) Make It Believable

The benefit you communicate in your headline needs to be believable. For example, you would never want to use a headline that said: "10 Ways To Guarantee You Make $Billions." Instead, you might rephrase it to state: "The 10 Tips Billionaires Credit For Making Their Billions."

7) Mention Your Niche

Oglivy suggests that if your advertising to a small group of people (e.g. men aged 65 and over), you should mention that in your headline. "New FDA-Approved Pill That Increases Erections For 90% Of Men Aged 65 & Over."

8) "Put Your Headline In Quotes"

Oglivy is a big fan of headlines in quotes and found they did 28% better than those without.

9) Mention Where They Live

If you're advertising in a local area, make sure to mention the location in the headline: "Introducing 24-Hour 5-Star Catering To San Francisco Businesses!" Notice how we included news ("Introducing"), self-interest/benefit ("5-Star Catering") and location all in the headline.

10) Three Things To Avoid In Headline Writing

There are some clear no-no's in writing headlines. Here are three:

Trickiness/Cleverness

In general, you want to avoid being too tricky or clever in a headline. While you want to pique a reader's curiosity, you don't want to completely puzzle them.

Caples gives the following example of a headline that is trying to be clever but fails to deliver enough benefit to get most people to read on:

"The Odds Are 9 To 1 Against You" (that was for a business training course). Most people won't keep reading the rest of the ad.

Little To No Headline At All

Some advertisements have no headline at all. Plain stupid. Similarly, some subject lines in emails say nothing or just "re:" or "fyi" — that's asking a lot from the reader and unless you two have a trusted, best-friend type relationship, you're going to get poor open rates of that email.

Gloom Or Negativity

In general, people don't want to be bummed out. If you're going to talk about something negative (e.g. you think the stock market is going to plunge) then try to turn it into the positive such as "7 Quick Tips To Protect Yourself From The Coming Wall Street Crash." Notice how the headline also uses curiosity.

Some examples of good headlines:

"They Laughed When I Sat Down At the Piano, But When I Started To Play!"

This headline (pictured on page 121) was written by John Caples himself! It shows clear benefit (everyone wants to be popular) and piques curiosity.

"56% Off Baseball Autographed By Buster Posey"

Groupon and its army of copywriters make the benefit crystal clear in the headline (aka subject lines) of their emails.

"Have You Ever Seen A Bald-Headed Sheep"

Oglivy loved this headline from Lanolin, for a cure for baldness, because it shows benefit and piques curiosity.

"Soup On The Rocks"

Another Oglivy favorite is a Campbell's Soup ad, which showed a clear benefit (taste) in a headline of just a few words.

Two must-reads to help you with headlines are: Tested Advertising Methods by John Caples and Oglivy On Advertising by David Oglivy

Effective Communication: The Higher The Sensitivity, The Higher The Bandwidth

Choose your communication channel wisely!

Cerner Corp. CEO Neal Patterson probably wished he had when he fired off a message to senior managers at his medical software maker berating them for their work habits.

Excerpts of the email include:

"The parking lot is sparsely used at 8 a.m.; likewise at 5 p.m....."

"...As managers — you either do not know what your EMPLOYEES are doing; or YOU do not CARE."

"You have a problem and you will fix it or I will replace you..."

"...What you are doing, as managers, with this company makes me SICK."

The e-mail promptly leaked out onto the Web. Two weeks after, Mr. Patterson sent the message, Cerner stock lost more than a quarter of its value (tens of millions of dollars) after investors became concerned about the company's prospects and employee morale.

That story reminded me that when you are communicating in business (or for any reason), that you should pick your communication medium based on the sensitivity of the topic. The higher the sensitivity, the higher the bandwidth of communication.

Here are four examples of channels of communication and their relative bandwidth

- In-Person (highest bandwidth) — Use this for your most sensitive topics.

- Telephone (medium bandwidth) — Use this as a backup for sensitive topics in the event you can't meet in-person with your audience.

- Instant Message (lower bandwidth) — Use this for lower-sensitivity topics.

- Email (lowest bandwidth) — Reserve this for your lowest-sensitivity topics (unless it's accompanied by a higher bandwidth in-person meeting)

Amazingly, Mr. Patterson is still CEO of Cerner today (8 years after the slip-up) — my hat is off to him for surviving such a firestorm. What a survivor! — And Cerner generated $188 million in pre-tax profit in its most recent year on sales of $1.67 billion so I imagine he is doing something right!

Bad News Is Good News (When It's Communicated)

Here's a valuable lesson I learned when I failed to communicate some bad news about a startup at which I was CEO. I made a bad executive hire for a company I was leading and decided, after speaking with some advisors, to terminate the relationship with the executive.

While the decision was sound, I failed to communicate this news (which some might perceive as "bad news") in a timely basis to one key person (an investor) who instead heard about it from one of my advisors within 24 hours.

That investor was so upset with me keeping this "bad news" from him that he called me into his office, threatened to take his investment money back and lectured me for two hours on how important it is to communicate bad news in the same way you communicate good news (quickly!).

Perception Outweighs Reality

The problem with what I had done: while my decision to dismiss the executive was sound, it was initially perceived as unsound by the investor due solely to the fact that I withheld the information from him. Perception in this case outweighed reality.

The investor said something that afternoon: "Bad News is Good News" — it's a weird phrase but it has stuck with me ever since.

There is a related excerpt from Jack Welch's book called Winning.

"Information you try to shut down will eventually get out and as it travels it will certainly morph, twist and darken."

He compares it to a really bad version of the children's game of "telephone."

Bad news is good news (when communicated effectively)!

How To Communicate During A Crisis

When you are in conflict- or crisis-mode, the tendency is to get emotionally charged and that sometimes leads to folks taking actions that are unhealthy for the business. Here are four steps that I adopted from the University of Maryland's Leadership Program to deal with communicating during crisis or conflict:

1) Separate the people from the problem

A good communication about conflict should focus on the underlying problem (not the person).

Two examples:

"We just discovered that we did not ship out products to certain customers over the last 10 days and now sales will be down 16% this month" (good)

"George (in shipping) slipped up and forgot to confirm that our shipping facility received our go-ahead to ship products out this month...and our sales are plummeting" (bad)

If you indeed do have a person-problem, then deal with the problem as a relationship problem by talking directly to the person you have a problem with (i.e. George)

2) Generate a variety of possible solutions before deciding what to do

Don't assume there is just one solution.

Example:

"After discussing this with all of you, we have two potential solutions: 1) Do nothing and just ship the customers their products late. 2) Send an apology email to each customer that their shipment will be late and that they will receive a bonus product as a thank you for their patience."

And it doesn't have to be your solution versus your team's solution.

3) Insist That Results Be Based On Some Objective Standard.

Examples:

- Efficiency

- Profitability

- Cash flow

- Ethics

That way, you and your team can measure how you get out of the crisis/conflict.

And if you're involved in a conflict and feeling angry about it, this Chinese Proverb has proven invaluable to many people:

"Never write when you're angry."

It's better to pause, collect your thoughts first and even talk to a colleague if you can...then start writing when you're calmer. Your communication will now be more effective.

Leadership

A Fun Way to Start Any Meeting: The "Awesomeness Report"

I've written a couple of articles on how to run a meeting (see the effective Daily Huddle, *page 139*, approach that the Ritz Carlton and others use or an easy 3-step framework in my G.A.P. Approach To Running Meetings, *page 96*, article). Over the last year I've added a fun way to START a meeting: "The Awesomeness Report."

It's real simple, I just ask the person I'm meeting with:

"What's something really awesome that's happened with you lately…in any part of your life."

I've found this to be a super-effective way to start a meeting because it virtually guarantees that you start off on a positive note (and "positive things happen to positive thinkers" as a wise man once said).

Some Awesome Things People Have Shared With Me In Recent Meetings

"My 18-year old son was chosen by his soccer teammates as one of the two most inspirational players on the team…and a good friend of mine's son was the other one chosen."

"My son just starred in the school play…and he killed it!"

"I just got back from Bogota, Columbia — a University there invited me to do 12 speeches (3 or 4 per day) and I got to travel around with a bodyguard and a translator!"

"I taught my two twin grand-daughters how to ride a bicycle...it was even more fun than teaching my son!"

"I'm going to a personal trainer the last 5 weeks...and I've lost 15 pounds."

"We were named Dell's agency of record."

"I just helped my Mom move out of our family home that she resided in for the last 37 years... a very cathartic experience...Mom is ecstatic!"

"I just jumped out of an airplane with my godson to celebrate his high school graduation last Saturday."

"My wife just got her law degree...and so we're both finally done with school!"

"My daughter just got back from spending her junior year abroad in Rome!"

"We (Crowdstar) just announced $23 million in funding!"

"I had my 20 year wedding anniversary and got remarried again (to the same husband) in a church wedding this time!"

"I went to Mexico for 5 days with a gorgeous Mexican woman...her parents own a lot of real estate...and we got to stay alone in the nicest house (in Punta Mita) that I've ever seen...with a staff of 8."

"I've decided to quit my job (as a venture capitalist) and run for mayor (of San Francisco)."

"My daughter just learned to read...and just like that...she now wants to read anything."

"We're on our third week of 2-hour training sessions for our team...so I can retire to the Caribbean one day!"

"I had this stock in an old Internet company and it was just sold to GenPact — so I have some found money!"

"I was finishing a triathlon the other day and my 5-year old daughter ran out towards the end of the race and said: 'I'm gonna beat you, daddy' — and then proceeded to beat her dad to the finish line."

I thought it was awesome when my friend's son Brennan so easily picked up my cat Fee (Fee did not find it as awesome).

"I just spent a week in Ireland for my grandma's 90th birthday (with my kids!)."

"I quit my job and decided to pursue my own startup."

"I went to Brazil recently and my son got to meet his grandfather for the first time."

"My little boy turned 5 years old and has an incredibly happy, fulfilling time at school and positive check-up at the doctor's."

"My younger brother just had his last day in classes in the New York City Fire Department."

"I found it awesome when my friend's daughter Lydia was so excited to show me her new pet rat."

"My business and I just got quoted in the Wall Street Journal!"

"We just sold our company…I think it's time for a new job!"

"I just quit my job (after 6 years) and I want to pursue new work in an emerging market like Vietnam or Ghana."

"I've had foot issues for awhile and this pilates instructor just helped me out — and now my foot feels great!"

"The new Transformers movie is coming out!"

"My daughter is now reading and playing the piano."

"I just got interviewed by Bloomberg's Game Changers TV show!"

"My son was just in a play about an island."

"I just built a content-generating tool that helps create unique content for each product in our database."

"Got a box at Hollywood Bowl (through his client) to see Phish when they come around."

Two other things about The Awesomeness Report:

1. It is an especially effective way to start a meeting with someone new...it's a great ice-breaker!

2. You have to be prepared to share your own awesomeness!

The Daily Huddle: How The Rockefeller's, Ritz Carlton And I Run Our Meetings

The Daily Huddle has arguably been one of the greatest productivity and efficiency boosters I've personally experienced. Since I started using it, I've run into numerous industry leaders (such as the Ritz Carlton and Johnson & Johnson) who benefit from the Daily Huddle. Duh, why didn't I begin this 20 years ago!

I first read about the concept of the Daily Huddle in Mastering the Rockefeller Habits, which may be the best how-to book for small businesses that I've read. Its author Verne Harnish was inspired by the habits of business tycoon John D. Rockefeller and translates those for you to apply to business today.

So, what is the Daily Huddle? Well, for starters, I use the term "Daily Huddle" because I like the ring of it — you may have heard it called names like Daily Scrum, Daily Pulse, Daily Agile, Daily Lineup (Ritz Carlton) or Daily StandUp. The concept is what counts.

BASICS

Let me outline the basics first:

- Time of day — It should be as early as possible (ideally in the morning).

- Length of time — 5 to 15 minutes (depending on the size of the team).

- Number of attendees — Teams of 7 or fewer people (if you have teams that are larger than 7, you probably have a team that needs to be split up).

- Who attends — Every person in your company should be attending at least one Daily Huddle (but no person should attend more than two or three).

- Who runs it — I recommend you pick the senior manager of the particular team to run it (unless he or she is not organized in which case pick the most senior organized person).

- Where does it take place — It can be done in person or over the phone or on videoconferencing if you're lucky enough to have one of those.

AGENDA

The agenda is the same every day. I recommend you first test out the Rockefeller Habits' suggested agenda. That's what I did and we didn't need to change a thing.

1. **What's Up** — The first section of the Daily Huddle should be about each of your team members sharing the What's Up of what they've accomplished since you all last met. Total time: 3 to 5 minutes (Every participant should talk for no more than 30 seconds each).

2. **The Numbers** — The second section is about the numbers of your business. Here, you should cover the critical metrics that are most important to your team. For example, in my sales Daily Huddle, we report on such vitals as total sales by brand from the previous day (with comparisons to prior periods) and percentage of our monthly sales goal we project. Total time: 3 to 5 minutes

3. **Roadblocks** — This section focuses on the roadblocks (also called "bottlenecks") that the team members face. Total time: 3 to 5 minutes.

4. **Values & Ideology** — This last section covers values-related items that don't fit nicely into the first 3 sections of the meeting. An example might be praise that someone outside the group has earned or a personal item that someone outside the meeting is facing that is affecting their performance (e.g., we just had a woman on our team whose neighborhood in Santa Barbara was on fire (from wildfires); and one of our values is to make sure to take care of such people in need of assistance (by offering to pick up her slack and be extra supportive of her and her family).

BONUS TIPS

Here are some other things I've noticed from my experience with the Daily Huddle.

- **Give it a Week** — It will be tough for your people to adopt at first (the first one will be awkward when, for instance, you ask people "What's Up?) — But it will become easier as the team figures it out (give it a good week!)

- **Don't Problem Solve** — You should keep it focused on problem-identification and not problem-solving (if there's a problem that can't be solved with a "one-liner" by one of the group, then you should schedule to meet off-line.

- **Start at an Odd Time** — Try scheduling it and a time other than the half-hour or hour (e.g. try 10:02am in the morning). Reason: People will remember it more and you'll find they show up at 10 a.m. to 10:01 a.m. (instead of being late!).

- **It Helps The Rest of Your Day** — The Daily Huddle will help you and your team better figure out how to spend the rest of their day.

- **Start with Senior People** — The most effective way to roll out the Daily Huddle is to have your organization's leaders do it first (*secret: if leaders do it, it will trickle down through the rest of your business*).

And please read Mastering the Rockefeller Habits — it's chock full of other valuable habits and ideas for businesses to grow.

5 Tips On How To Become A Top Innovator!

I was fascinated by the Harvard Business Review (HBR) Innovator's DNA article (an abstract is here with the option to purchase).

They researched such innovators as Apple's Steve Jobs, Amazon's Jeff Bezos, eBay's Pierre Omidyar and Meg Whitman, Intuit's Scott Cook and Proctor & Gamble's A.G. Lafley. Their key finding was that innovative entrepreneurs (who are also CEOs) spend 50% more time on five "discovery activities" than do CEOs with no track record for innovation. I fully agree with these five tips for how to innovate; and want to provide my insights on them:

Five Tips On How To Innovate

1) Question (The Status Quo)

HBR points out that Michael Dell famously created Dell with the question: "Why do computers cost five times the cost of the sum of their parts?" Innovators are excellent at asking questions that challenge the status quo such as:

- Why not try it this way?

- Why do you do things the way you do?

- What if you tried this new thing or stopped doing some old thing?

- What would you do if failure was not an option?

2) Observe

Innovators are strong at observing people and details. A great example that I heard about 20 years ago came from Scott Cook, the founder of Intuit (Quicken, Quickbooks, TurboTax).

Scott observed his wife spending a good deal of time writing checks and decided that the laborious process of writing checks could be highly automated through a simple process through which you type in the fields of a check (using an actual graphical depiction of a check) on your computer.

Scott also used to hang out at the computer stores and follow people who bought his Quicken product outside and ask them if he could "observe" them as they install the software and get their feedback so that he could further innovate.

Steve Jobs: A Master of Observing

Another example of an innovator "observing" would be Steve Jobs' famous visit to Xerox Labs where he observed a number of new Xerox developments such as the graphical user interface (which led to the Macintosh) and laser printing technology (which led to Apple's Laser Printers (which were hugely popular in their time).

Jeff Bezos said something a few years back that also comes under this category of observing: he said that if you want to get ideas for new things to create then "watch the hobbyists." It is often the hobbyist/techie/geek person who is playing around with things that can be turned into breakthrough products.

3) Experiment (aka "Test")

Thomas Edison went through 2,000 tests to find a filament for an efective light bulb and examined 17,000 plant species to come up with a new synthetic rubber. Few of us will experiment like Edison, so here's a more recent example using the most powerful testing platform in our lifetime — the Internet:

Timothy Ferris, author of The Four Hour Work Week (one of my favorite books!) ran a test to come up with the title of his book. He placed Adwords text ads, varied the titles, and chose the title with the highest click-thru rate. "The 4 Hour Workweek," which wasn't his favorite, won.

This brings to mind Proctor & Gamble's famous philosophy that "Our most important products are our failures."

4) Network

To be able to effectively observe, question and test things, it sure helps innovators to be a good networker — after all, if you're keeping mostly to yourself you simply won't have the information, knowledge or data that you could gather through others. HBR points out that David Neeleman created the key ideas for JetBlue at networking conferences and Michael Lazaridis was inspired to found Research in Motion (creators of the Blackberry) at a conference in 1987.

And as you're coming up with new ideas for a startup, I fully agree with entrepreneur Chris Dixon's approach that you keep track of all of your ideas in a spreadsheet and show them to as many smart people as you can find — read his Developing New Startup Ideas posting for how he does this. If you need help with networking, check out my networking articles.

5) Associate (aka "Connect")

Finally, Associating (or connecting) is a skill that allows people to make connections across seemingly unrelated ideas, questions, data, problems and opportunities. This is arguably the most important skill because it's required to connect problems or ideas in ways that haven't been before.

Steve Jobs is known to refer to this as "connecting" - -indeed it's Mr. Jobs who illustrates my favorite example of Associating/Connecting. Jobs made a connection between the demand for music on the Internet (as witnessed by the explosive growth of the use of the Napster Music service on the Web) with the trend of greater storage in mobile devices (specifically, the minimization of hard drives to enable 1,000 songs to fit on a drive the size of a pack of gum).

Thus the iPod was born. I hope this helps you innovate more in life...isn't that what life is all about...creating and growing!?

7 Tips On How To Motivate Your Team Through Feeling "Progress"

A feeling of "progress" may be the most important motivator for you or your team, according to a Harvard Business Review study on what motivates people (thanks to my colleague Mary Rosenberger for pointing this one out). The HBR study took an interesting angle on motivation by studying hundreds of workers and digging into what happens on a great work day.

The gist of the study is that on days when workers feel like they're making progress on projects their emotions are positive and that increases their drive to succeed. The opposite is true: when workers are feeling like they're on the "hamster wheel," working hard with little in the way of results, they feel negative emotions and their performance plummets. And the progress that your team feels can even be small...and they'll still feel motivated!

7 Tips For How To Motivate Your Team Through Progress

1) Set SMART Goals

- **S**pecific — Well defined, clear to everyone

- **M**easurable — There should be a metric or some measurement to identify how you're progressing on your goal.

- **A**greed-Upon — The goal should be agreed upon by the people working on it.

- **Realistic** — The goal can be ambitious but should be within reason.

- **Time-based** — Every goal should have a time-line.

2) Provide Resources Necessary to Achieve Goals

You as a leader should do whatever you can to provide the resources necessary for your team to work on reaching goals. Spend one-on-one time with them to discuss the goals and ask them what they need to reach them.

3) Hold Frequent Meetings To Chunk Down Goals

Let's say you've got your team's quarterly goals in place. Now you're going to want to set up frequent meetings within the quarter to discuss them. I recommend that you meet with your team either daily (or every other day) (see Daily Huddle from page 139).

In those huddles, ask your direct report to list things that they could do in THAT WEEK to make progress on the quarterly priorities.

Example of chunking down the quarterly goal:

- If it's the beginning of the quarter, the first week's goal may be as simple as committing to identifying the 10 Fortune 100 customers your direct report is going to go after.

- The following week's goal may be to telephone a contact at each of the ten Fortune 100 customers.

- In the week after that, your direct report may agree to commit to making a proposal to a certain Fortune 100 customer.

Now, as your direct report makes headway on these chunked-down goals, they will have a feeling of progress. Remember this nugget of wisdom from my business hero Coach John Wooden (I'm paraphrasing): Progress is not necessarily reaching your goal...progress is working as hard as you reasonably can on your goal and then letting the results be what they may.

4) Celebrate Milestones

When you reach your goals (i.e. milestones), take a moment to celebrate. Acknowledge each and every person involved in the project...ideally with specifics on what they contributed to its success. As a CEO, I ask my team to remind me of whenever anyone does something impressive...and then I try to write a quick congratulatory note to that team member (cc:ing their manager).

5) Acknowledge Failure As Progress

Don't forget that failure is progress. For example, your team may have a goal of trying to close certain types of customers or partnerships. If you explore one such deal and it's not a good fit (for you or the other party), that is still progress.

6) Be Authentic

This one's easy: your praise of people should always be authentic. Don't tell someone they "really moved the ball forward" when you actually don't know what they did.

7) Be Decisive

If you as a leader are indecisive about decisions around goals and priorities then you delay the feeling of progress that your team gets when they either reach (or fail to reach) their goal.

Progress is tough to feel when leadership is wishy-washy. So be decisive about such things as:

- Setting goals

- Providing resources to help the goals get reached

- Pulling the plug on deals/losing deals (once in awhile you will either want to pull the plug on a deal or you will have it pulled for you by another party — this is ok, just make it fast).

If you can work on the above 7 tips, you will help motivate your team though progress.

7 Signs That Your Boss Is A Charisma-Based Narcissistic Leader

Few things irk me more than hearing from friends who have to work with "narcissistic leaders." Why would my friends work with someone who's "narcissistic?" Because they are charismatic — they are able to mobilize resources (i.e. you and others!) through their charisma.

I call such leaders "Charisma-Based Narcissistic Leaders." Gordon Gekko is an excellent example of a "Charisma-Based Narcissistic Leader" The scary part is that these charismatic leaders usually meet 2 of the 3 requirements that Warren Buffett demands in a good business person (high intelligence and high energy) — it's the third one (high integrity) they have a problem with (see Warren Buffett's 3 Simple Steps On Who To Hire for more on that). Ok, so on with it — here are 7 signs that you work with one of these jackasses:

1) They're Big On Titles (Especially They're Own)

Narcissistic leaders typically love big titles...and even more than one! For example, you might find them using:

- Founder, Chairman & CEO (instead of just CEO) or

- Vice President & General Manager (instead of just VP)

And don't be surprised to see your Charisma-Based Narcissistic Leaders holding multiple positions OUTSIDE your organization. One look at their LinkedIn profile and you might see a few other positions they hold (even if they aren't that active in them). These toxic leaders tend to LOVE acquiring titles that show their authority — ego is a major driver of this.

2) They Take Credit For Your Work

Charisma-based leaders are amazingly talented at taking credit for your work. This may happen internally (e.g. you solve a problem and your leader implies to their peers or manager that they solved the problem themselves).

Or it may happen externally: a press release goes out about an achievement and it's your ego-driven leader's name that's on it (not the main driver of the achievement). You ever hear the advice smart folks give about "NOT having pride of authorship" about a product (i.e. be a team player)? Well, your toxic leader DOES have pride of ownership — their own!

3) They Revise History To Their Benefit (aka "Revisionist History")

A charisma-based narcissistic leader often practices revisionist history. For example, you may have warned them that some system would fail unless it was upgraded ...and they don't follow your recommendation. And when the system later fails, they point the finger at you and say: "Why did you let this happen!?"

This can happen with positive events too — an idea that you suggested ends up working and they later on say something to the effect of: "I'm glad we executed MY idea."

4) They Care More About *Their* Team Than *Your* Team

Narcissistic leaders often have an "Us Versus Them" philosophy in their organization where:

- Us = them and their direct reports

- Them = your team

So they may care about you as you serve their team but they don't really care about you as part of YOUR OWN team.

What can make this extra-frustrating is that they will sometimes micro-manage and go directly to someone on your team (around your back)…but only to serve their own interests (not your own or your team's).

They also tend to manage up a lot better than they manage down. It's just awful!

5) They Put In Place Corporate Structures That Don't Make Sense

Charisma-Based Narcissistic Leaders are so blinded by their own ego that they will change the structure of your organization in ways that don't make sense. Some examples:

- People on the team may have multiple bosses (usually a bad idea)

- People will report to your leader when they should really be reporting to someone else.

- Changes and surprises are typically negative events for those involved.

6) They Appear To Be More Of An Actor Than Real Person

Friends of mine describe their narcissistic bosses as "putting on a show" about their thoughts or feelings on business matters. Speaking of putting on a show, your narcissistic boss may often dress the part — wearing expensive high-status types of outfits and driving an over-the-top car. Their authenticity is very hard to judge.

7) Constructive Criticism (Of Them) Is Not Welcome

Charisma-based narcissistic leaders may like to dish out criticism but they have a hard time hearing it themselves. Those around them walk on egg-shells. This creates more of the "us versus them" environment in which you're either with your narcissistic boss or you're against them.

Determining A Person Is A Charisma-Based Narcissistic Leader BEFORE You Work With Them

In an ideal world, you don't ever end up working for a charisma-based narcissistic boss. Here are some signs that you may be able to catch ahead of time, before you even work with one of these people.:

- They use "I" or "Me" or "My" much more than "We" or "Us" or "Our."

- They have little to no self-awareness

- They have large networks of contacts (yet few high-integrity people who work with them more than once)

And if it's too late, and you work with one of these toxic bosses already, my only advice is: "Get out now...and fast!"

Business Is Like A Decathlon: Be Decent At These 10 Things And You'll Win The Gold

The Olympic decathlon — a combined event of 10 different track and field races — is a perfect metaphor for business.

You don't have to win every one of the 10 races in the Olympic decathlon to win the gold - in fact, you can win the decathlon without being the best at any of the 10 races.

Bruce Jenner (winner of the 1976 Olympic Decathlon) averaged the equivalent of little better than 3rd place in each race — and he still won the decathlon by a substantial margin. Inspired by the decathlon metaphor, here is a 10-item checklist for succeeding in business...if you train to place in these 10 business races, you can win the business gold.

1) VISION

As I wrote in my blog on 3 Tips On How To Write A Good Vision Statement, a vision statement is key to starting your business. It helps you and your team answer the question:

"Am I working on what's right for the organization?"

Don't you think the Ben & Jerry's team has a clear idea of how to delight customers when they read their terrific vision: "Making the best possible ice cream, in the nicest possible way"

Go check out 40 more of my favorite vision statement examples (some are mission statements/taglines) for inspiration for your own vision.

2) BUSINESS MODEL

You have to gain mastery of your business model to successfully start a new business. I know one entrepreneur who has 3 million unique visitors to his Web site each month but makes no money...and he's in panic mode.

You might say that you'd love to be in that situation (after-all, can't the guy just sell his Web site?) — well, it's not that easy when you have overhead (his salary and contract fees for a few others and hosting fees) to pay and you're losing money every month.

As Warren Buffett says: "Rule number one in business: never lose money. Rule number two: never forget rule number one."

Check out Skill #2 in The 5 Core Skills Every CEO Should Have or How Much To Pay For A Customer or 5 Steps To Inevitability Thinking (How To Make It Inevitable That You'll Generate $20K Per Mo. In Ad Revenue) to get some ideas on mastering your business model.

Even if you're giving away some or all of your product for free, you should have mastery over the Freemium business model as I wrote about in It's The Freeconomy, Stupid: Free As A $300B Business Model.

3) MOBILIZING RESOURCES

You must be above average at mobilizing resources to succeed in business. Examples of things you should be able to do in the early days of a business include:

- Talk a couple of people into working on your new business for free

- Talk your law firm into deferring all of your startup legal expenses

- Talk your wealthy family & friends into giving you some seed money

- Talk other Web sites into linking to you

- Talk friends or colleagues into introducing you to the very best experts at the 10 things I list in this article! (i.e. you need to be hanging around the best in order for you to be above average)

A key part of mobilizing resources is networking (one of my favorite things!) as I write about in these articles on business networking.

4) CONNECTING THINGS

I was thrilled when Harvard Business Review included "Connecting" (aka: Associating) in its list of top criteria that every business innovator should have.

Building a successful business (or product) is about connecting things. Here's an example I gave on page 143 of Steve Jobs connecting from How To Innovate: 5 Tips From The Top Innovators: Indeed it's Mr. Jobs who illustrates my favorite example of Associating/ Connecting.

Jobs made between the demand for music on the internet (as witnessed by the explosive growth of the use of the Napster Music service on the Web) with the trend of greater storage in mobile devices (specifically, the minimization of hard drives to enable 1,000 songs to fit on a drive the size of a pack of gum). Thus the iPod was born. What are 2 or 3 things that you are uniquely qualified to connect to produce the next iPod!?

5) MARKETING

If you aren't actively thinking about the following questions, you're not yet an above-average marketer or entrepreneur:

- What problem are you solving (Facebook allows friends to more easily share stuff)?

- What opportunity are you presenting (e.g. typing out 140 characters of text to friends and strangers (Twitter))?

- What makes for a good advertisement?

- What makes for a good headline? (learn this in 5 minutes by reading 10 Easy Tips On How To Write Better Headlines on page 121)

- What makes for a good name (whether for a product, project or company)?

6) SELLING

I don't care how good your business idea is, if you can't sell it you're toast. You don't have to be "salesy" like a real estate agent or used car salesman…but you have to be able to ask for (and take) the order! For a 5-minute lesson on what's important in selling, go read How To Sell Better: The Simple 4-Step Spin-Selling Approach.

And this starts with yourself — when you're first starting a business, the most important thing you will need to sell is you!

7) PSYCHOLOGY (Especially Empathy)

Building a business always comes down to humans…either humans you're managing or humans you're trying to market or sell to or humans you're partnering with…I think you get it.

A good entrepreneur needs to put themselves in another human's shoes…understand their psyche. In short, you need to be good at empathy. Read my Psychology articles or some of the mental models like Incentives, Parkinson's Law, Pavlovian Association, Scarcity or Self-Interest in Charlie Munger's Mental Models to get some primers on psychology.

8) COMMUNICATION

It's cliché: you gotta be good at communication to succeed in business. Well, some clichés are indeed true!

But let's break down where you need to be strong:

- **Writing** — You should be able to write succinctly (e.g. in an email, your subject line is clear and the body of your message is well structured with a clear call to action/response at the end). Check out How To Write An Effective Email on page 119 or 7 Tips For Writing Like Warren Buffett on page 115.

- **Speaking** — You need to be a decent public speaker (whether it's in front of potential recruits, your team, potential customers, etc.) — I recommend Toastmasters or other public speaking to everyone.

- **Listening** — "He who listens most, wins," as paraphrased from Art of War.

If you want to dig deep into how to communicate better in business, check out my articles on Communication.

9) SPEED & ITERATION

Just like the 100-meters decathletes must run, a good entrepreneur needs to be quick/fast. But that doesn't mean you have to rush things. As a hero of mine John Wooden liked to day: "Be quick, but don't rush."

To grow your business you need to move super-fast in creating things, examine the results and then iterate. There are numerous tips to increasing your speed: one is using the Daily Huddle on page 138 in your business meetings; another is to chunk down your goals as I wrote about in The 10 Maniacal Steps I Use To Set Goals on page 50.

10) PATIENCE & LONGEVITY

While being quick (#9 above) is key to a successful business, don't forget the main message of Aesop's tale of the tortoise and hare: "Slow and steady wins the race."

I'm fortunate: my dad and Buffett have been constant reminders to me of this. As Buffett says: "Someone's sitting in the shade today because someone planted a tree a long time ago."

Ninety percent of startups fail and my unscientific opinion is that the vast majority of them do so because they run out of time/money. Always ask yourself: "How can I buy my business more time?"

With time, comes additional opportunity. It took 9 years before my startup Mojam was sold (and part of the reason we were able to sell it was because we just stuck around).

The great Google is known to value longevity too. Just ask anyone who has run a Web site for more than a couple of years...they'll tell you that there comes a point where you don't even have to do much updating to your site (e.g. a blog) and Google will send you additional traffic (because longevity is part of Google's algorithm).

Two key ways to buy yourself more time and execute a long-term business:

- Create profits as soon as you can (if you have positive cash-flow, you don't have to rush!)

- Raise money — check out The 7 Unusual Fundraising Lessons I Learned While Raising $1 Million+ on page 108.

If you can be above average at these 10 business races, your chances for starting and succeeding in business greatly improve.

7 Business Lessons I Learned From The Grateful Dead

I'm a big fan of the Grateful Dead — I attended 100+ shows, collected 300+ bootlegs (that are in cassette form still in the hallway of my San Francisco apartment!) and I received an original signed 1968 Grateful Dead concert poster as a signing bonus when I sold the my Mojam business.

In additional to bringing me a bunch of musical joy, The Dead taught me a ton about my other passion: business. Just look at the numbers: The Dead pulled in $95 million a year at the height of their 30+ year journey (according to Booz & Co.) and were referred to by The Altantic Magazine as "one of the most profitable bands in the history of music" (see Management Secrets of The Grateful Dead article).

7 Business Lessons I Learned From The Grateful Dead

1) Moving the "Free Line"

There's a lot of talk in Internet business these days about "moving the free line" — in other words, providing more of your products/value available for free and make your money on the back-end. Well the Grateful Dead were doing this 40 years ago.

The Dead made much of their product (their music) free by allowing fans to make recordings at their shows — they even set up a "taper section" dedicated to the fans who were recording so that all of their tall microphones and other equipment could be conveniently placed in one part of the concert venue.

Those recordings were of course copied and shared amongst many fans (both those who attended that particular show and those who didn't) and acted as free viral marketing for the band (I had 50 bootlegs of the Grateful Dead before I even attended my first show!). So, let's take me as a customer for instance: the Grateful Dead didn't have any of my money for the first year of my exposure to their products.

The Dead were pushing the concept of "moving the free line" 40 years before this best selling book on the subject. But by the time I attended my first show (October 12, 1983 at Madison Square Garden in New York City) I was hooked as a customer– and would invest many thousands of dollars on additional live shows, t-shirts and recordings over the next 12 years.

Think about it: Would you allow me to have some of your products for free for a year if you knew I would be a loyal customer paying you $5,000 for additional products over the following decade (and turn on a number of my friends who would also invest around the same!?). I think so!

2) Product First, Profit Later

Sam I. Hill, Chief Marketing Officer of Booz-Allen & Company in Chicago, points out that the Grateful Dead were leaders in the "Product First/Profit Later" philosophy later executed by Nike, IAMS Pet Foods, Snap-On Tools and MTV — (e.g. Nike set out to build a better running shoe; IAMS, a high-quality pet food) in this "How to Truck The Brand: Lessons from the Grateful Dead" article from 1997.

Hill added: These companies simply believed in what they were doing and "were smart enough to see when it worked, and to exploit it."

One former president of the Grateful Dead, Ron Rakow (whose cool business card from the time is here) is an uncle of a friend of mine. Ron once told me a relevant story that I'll do my best to paraphrase: Rakow said that early on in the Spring of 1967 he asked the band (before the band was successful) what they envisioned success looking like. A few of the band members responded with such comments as:

- "I want to have a number one record;"

- "I want to have a number one hit;" and

- "I want us to be famous"

But Jerry Garcia, the band's unofficial leader, said something more to the effect of: "That all sounds good, but I think we'd just like to have as many people as possible enjoy our music."

Rakow told me at this point that all the band members nodded their heads in agreement with Jerry, saying "Yes, yes, ...lots of people should listen to our music — that's it!"

As Rakow tells it, the band then agreed to empty all the money out of their pockets (there was a total of $50 or so) and rent a flat-bed truck on which they would play a free live concert in the Panhandle near Golden Gate Park in San Francisco).

The band indeed put on a free show on May 28, 1967 in the Panhandle...Rakow says that initially very few people showed up but the band kept playing for a few hours and eventually many thousands of people joined in.

...and the Grateful Dead product was on its way (with profits very soon to follow).

3) Secret to Being #1: Do NOT Be The Best At What You Do...

Music Promoter Bill Graham famously described the Grateful Dead on the Marquee of the Warfield Theatre in San Francisco as: "They're not the best at what they do, they're the only ones that do what they do."

I think you get it? Focus on what is truly unique about you or your business...and then OWN that! Examples of the uniqueness of the Grateful Dead included:

- Making up the set list every night — They operated without a set list most nights

- NOT playing their biggest hits every night — They repeated songs live (including their most popular) only once every 4+ shows

- Creating their own music category — Because they blended so many musical styles — rock, country, bluegrass, jazz, funk, R&B, reggae and more! — The Dead were impossible to put into a category...so, guess what: the world created a new one for them: called either "Jam Bands" or just simply "Grateful Dead type music"

- Being the first band to play at the Pyramids in Egypt — The Dead invested $500,000 to visit Egypt and play at the Pyramids and donated the proceeds to local organizations within Cairo (the final night's performance was capped off by a full moon and total lunar eclipse)

- Using two drummers — Hardly any top rock bands were using two drummers. One of them, Micky Hart, played an unusual 11-count measure to his drumming

- "Spacing" Out — Every night, the band would play music with no words for about 20 minutes (this was called "Drums/Space"

- Recording when they felt like it — They were known to go into the recording studio only when they felt like it. I've heard Garcia admit that they simply weren't very good studio musicians — live music was their strength!

I can't tell you how they came up with such unique approaches as above...but if I had to put money on it, I'd bet that these things happened organically, played to their uniqueness/strengths or that they did it just for the hell of it.

One thing's for sure: they did NOT conform to the industry norms!

4) Embrace Your Community

The Dead invested a bunch in their community. I already mentioned the taping they allowed, which helped build a massive community that they could not easily reach on their own.

Another example of community was that they allowed fans to mail in requests for tickets (as opposed to relying on buying tickets from a ticket seller like Ticketmaster) (there was also a Dead hotline). This gave Dead fans a feeling of connection with the band (as in, we kind of know where they live).

Other examples of the Dead's support of community included the Parking Lot scene at shows. The Dead allowed vending in one part of the parking lot (which Deadheads called "Shakedown Street) and many people made their living selling t-shirts, bagels, grilled cheese and pizza.

One friend of mine sold $70,000 per year in pizzas at Grateful Dead concerts! And the Dead embraced it! The band eventually brought these vendors in as official licensees, according to Booz & Co.

The Dead also embraced fans making money from small community projects such as Deadbase, a print out of every concert the band ever played with the setlist of songs, that some people sold (such information is now free). The Dead was constantly testing cool new things for its community.

I remember walking up to their sound engineer Dan Healy at a 1986 show in Pittsburgh, PA and he explained how they were testing out emitting a radio signal from their soundboard of each show — so that people could listen to the show on their radio.

I tested it out and it was amazing: I was inside a concert listening to an FM Walkman with higher-quality audio than I was hearing within the arena itself. And the fans in the parking lot (who didn't have tickets to the show) were even more excited that they could hear the show with nothing more than a radio (for free!).

5) Organized Chaos: "Grateful Google?"

A big buzzword in business strategy these days is "Organized Chaos" — Google may be the true master of the concept. Examples of Google's chaos: employees can decorate their offices however they want, ride around offices on scooters and goof off on company time and the founders have a "we'll do what we want, whenever we feel like it" attitude.

However, Google is highly organized/structured: Google breaks down most teams into small groups with two engineers co-running them; the recommended allocation of goof-off time is 10% and the entire company is behind Google's mission of organizing the world's information (through the most vast server farms in the world).

Talk About Organized Chaos? Here's Google's First Production Server to Organize the World's Information (source: Steve Jurvetson via Wikipedia).

But long before Google it was the Grateful Dead who were laying down the magic formula for Organized Chaos.

I probably don't have to spend much time explaining the chaotic part of the Dead (picture the band showing up in their t-shirts and jeans jamming out to whatever setlist they felt like that night with their avid tie-dyed clothed fans twirling around in circles (many of them under the influence of LSD).

But in actuality, there was a lot of organization to the Grateful Dead:

- **Touring** — They consistently toured 50 to 100 shows per year (including a Spring & Fall Tour) in four regions with very specific dates and locations/venues.

- **Sets of Their Shows** — Almost all of their shows were structured into two sets with 5 to 10 songs in each set, followed by an encore.

- **Drums/Space** — The second set of almost all shows (from the mid-1970s on) included a section in the middle called "Drums/Space" in which the percussionists jammed out alone for a while and then the rest of the band noodled around with non-song music. While Drums/Space was highly chaotic at times (check out this 1987 show (with some cool visual graphics), it was predictably timed in the concert with a handful of songs before and after it.

- **Distributed Management** — The Dead's band members (and some crew) rotated as CEOs on a regular basis — how's that for sharing accountability!?

Long before Silicon Valley coined the phrase "Co-Opetition" (the concept of cooperating with your competition), The Dead made it a key part of their movement.

1. They invited bands who were competing for the Deadhead customer base — including Phish and The Dave Matthews Band — to be their warm-up band for concerts.

2. They openly invited competing musicians, such as Carlos Santana and Pete Townshend, to join them onstage to strut their stuff.

3. They played cover songs of many other bands such as The Beatles, Rolling Stones and Bob Marley) whose products were still marketed at the Deadhead demographic.

This had the effect of keeping such rival music closer within the Grateful Dead "orbit." After all, if you could get a bit of The Beatles, The Stones or The Who as part of your Grateful Dead experience, isn't the Grateful Dead orbit even more powerful!?

7) Reinvent Yourself

While the Grateful Dead's leader Jerry Garcia died August 9, 1995, their music and business lessons live on with members of the original Grateful Dead playing in such bands as The Dead, Phil Lesh & Friends, Bob Weir, Ratdog, Rhythm Devils, 7 Walkers and Further.

It's a testament to the powerful momentum of the Grateful Dead, that numerous successful bands emerged from the ashes of the death of its de-facto leader. And the business innovations from these Grateful Dead spinoffs keep comin'.

Marcom Professional's Marketing lessons from the Grateful Dead points to his recent experience with the spin-off band The Dead:

- They continue to sell tickets directly to fans (they are one of the few bands who can bypass Ticketmaster)

- They sell recordings of any of their new shows at The Grateful Dead Store

- They sell a print book customized for ANY show customers want

So, 45 years after the Grateful Dead were founded, the band's enterprise value "keeps on truckin onnnnn, on."

I hope you leverage these tips to design your business to last that long!

The Pros & Cons (10 Each) Of Leading A Virtual Business

I worked on the management team of Hot Topic Media, purely virtual company — as in, we don't have any physical office.

At about 70 people, Hot Topic is one of the largest purely virtual companies I know of.

Leading a remote team of people comes with its benefits and challenges – here are ones I experienced:

Benefits of a Virtual Business

1. **You Can Hire Best of Breed** — Arguably the most valuable benefit of working remotely is that you can hire THE best person for a role (as opposed to settling on hiring in a specific region).

2. **Physically Healthier** — Your team has the potential to lead a more healthy lifestyle if they work virtually as they'll have more opportunity to exercise and they will also likely eat more meals made by themselves (which are typically smaller/healthier portions) — I recommend that you emphasize to your team to take advantage of this opportunity!

3. **Lower Overhead** — You save the cost of renting, leasing or owning physical property.

4. **More Flexible Scheduling for Your Team** — Your team can have a little more flexibility for determining their working hours; for example, if a team member wants to take off a half-

day of work on Friday and then make up for the work on a Saturday afternoon, that becomes easier.

5. **No Commute Time** — Your virtual team has the potential to work more hours than they would in an office, since they won't be commuting, this will also save them commuting costs (car, bus, train, etc.).

6. **Lighter Carbon Footprint** — Your virtual team will be producing fewer greenhouse gas emissions per person.

7. **More Time With Children** — Your team can see their children (or pets) more often.

8. **Metrics Become Dominant** — My experience is that a virtual environment has an interesting positive bi-product: you will need to utilize metrics even more than usual (since you won't be able to see as much in-person proof of results)...this is a good thing.

9. **Increased Travel Opportunity** — Allowing your team to work virtually means that if they have the proper setup, they can work from different locations (allowing them to travel to new and exciting places that will help them grow)

10. **The Team Saves Money on Food** — Your team will likely spend less on food when they work from home.

Challenges of a Virtual Business

1. **Difficult to Express Emotions** — It's way more difficult to read emotions in a virtual work environment — for example, if a person is about to cry, you can not as easily tell that over the phone that you can in person.

2. **Difficult to Visually Represent Thoughts** — It is tougher to represent information virtually than in person. A giant white-board is way more efficient for communicating than any Web application I know of.

3. **Tougher to Post Job Listings** — Many job posting sites — including Craigslist and LinkedIn — do not let you do a job

posting to the whole world (they force you to name a geographic area)

4. **People Can Hide Things More Easily: More Difficult to Hold Accountable** — In general, you will have to work harder to hold people accountable when you're working virtually — it's just much easier for someone to "drop the ball" virtually than it is for them to do so in person.

5. **Physical Dormancy** — Watch out for your sitting posture. Working from home typically means that your body will be in a static seated position longer than if you were going into an office (since going into an office means you'll typically be taking more walks to conference rooms, restrooms, outdoor breaks).

6. **Street Noise** — You may find more street noise working at home. For instance, I work in my home, which is one-story up on a relatively quiet street yet I still have construction work outside, yard work by neighbors and couriers buzzing my doorbell.

7. **Time Zone Management** — You will typically have more of your people spread across multiple time zones which means some creative scheduling. In the case of our management team, for instance, we have three of us in the Pacific Standard Zone (PST) and two others in the Eastern Standard Zone (PST); which is three hours apart.

8. **No High-Five's** — I have learned that physically connecting with a team member — whether through a hug or a high-five — is helpful to team bonding...you have much less opportunity for celebrating small wins in a virtual environment.

9. **Fewer Opportunities to Bond Away From Work** — When your team is working remotely, you will have fewer opportunities to bond outside of work because: A) There may be more of a physical distance between your homes and B) You won't have a mutual office in which you can say: "Let's go grab a drink together after work" or "take a jog together during lunch break."

10. **You'll Have To Work Harder At Communication** — Effective communication in business is always vital; as you work in virtual environment, you will want to err on the side of over-communication to make sure your team is as much on the same page as feasible.

Bonus Tips for Virtual Environments

- **Virtual Team Communication Tools**

    o **Skype** — Effective for free two-person video conferencing calls

    o **Google Docs/Apps** — We use the Enterprise Version of Google Apps/Docs and are pleased with the collaboration abilities

    o **Screen sharing** — We use Microsoft's Live Meeting to show our desktops to each other

    o **FreeConferenceCall.com** — We use this Web site to set up free conference calls

- **Managing Virtual Teams**

    o **Daily Huddle** — Just about every person on the team is involved in some type of daily huddle with their team (ideally 7 or fewer people) (see The Daily Huddle article I wrote on page 138.

    o **Team Calls** — We do a conference call with the entire company on a bi-weekly (every two weeks) basis (we cover general updates and training)

    o **Ask "How do you feel?" more often** — I find it useful to ask our team how they feel more often than I would in an in-person work environment. This is especially important for the "Feelers" on your team.

    o **Introverts** — For the more quiet introverted people on our team, I try to get them more involved by asking them their opinion on conference calls.

○ **Regular in-person get-togethers (including for Strategic Planning)** — I've found it useful to get our smaller teams (e.g. our Management Team) together in person on a regular basis (quarterly or monthly is ideal if you can afford it) — in person meetings are most effective for Strategic Planning meetings (such as setting 3 year plans, 2-year plans, 1-year plans, etc.) where you need to do exercises such as a SWOT Analysis.

Another important lesson I found is that working in a virtual workplace tends to be really easy when your business is performing well and super-difficult when your business is having performance challenges.

That means that you're really going to have to be at the top of your game during the tough times.

How To Easily Craft An Awesome Vision Statement

Do vision statements really make a difference?

It's fascinating to look at the vision of two very successful companies — who competed from their early days...and see how things turned out:

Microsoft Versus Apple On Vision:

Bill Gates of Microsoft had this vision at about 30 years old:

"A computer on every desktop."

And Steve Jobs of Apple had this vision around the same time:

"A computer in the hands of everyday people."

Isn't it interesting how things turned out!?

Microsoft's Vision was focused on *volume*: "A computer on *every* desktop."

And sure enough Microsoft ended up with their products on *the most* desktops in the world – they achieved dominant market share!

And Apple's Vision was more focused on *quality/usability* — "...in the hands of *everyday* people."

Most people would agree that Apple's products are among the most usable in the world – I recommend them to my mom!

Microsoft went after quantity; Apple went after quality.

A Business Starts With A Vision

If you're involved in starting any business creation, the very first thing I recommend you figure out is the wording of your vision.

What is a vision statement?

My definition: A vision statement is a single sentence that explains clearly and specifically what it is you or your business is trying to create in the future.

3 Tips To Help You Craft A Vision Statement

1) A Good Vision Statement Is Concise

When Sergey Brin and Larry Page walked into Sequoia Capital's offices to ask for an investment into their new startup Google, they explained their vision in these words:

"To provide access to the world's information in one click."

Those 10 words were so key to Sequoia's investment in Google, that Sequoia now requires all of its entrepreneurs to have a vision statement of 10 or fewer words before they even get a meeting with Sequoia.

Note: While I don't recommend you get hung up on your vision statement being 10 words or less, I have noticed that the best vision statements are 15 or fewer words (see Vision Statement examples below).

2) A Good Vision Statement Is Specific

On May 25, 1961, U.S. President John F. Kennedy gave a speech to Congress in which he said:

"I believe that this nation should commit itself to achieving the goal, before this decade is out, of landing a man on the Moon and returning him safely to Earth."

Look at how specific JFK was:

Goal: Man on the moon (and back safely)

Time Frame: By the end of the decade

On July 21st, 1969, Neil Armstrong and Buzz Aldrin stepped on the moon and three days later the Apollo 11 crew returned safely to Earth.

3) A Good Vision Statement Answers The Question: "Are We Working On The Right Thing?"

If you're working at Disney Land (perhaps dressed as Donald Duck) and you're faced with a crying kid or upset parent, does this Disney Vision Statement help them figure out what to do:

"To make people happy."

I think it sure does!

How about if you're an employee on the team at Amazon, and someone suggests the aggressive idea of same-day shipments of products to customers?

Is that consistent with Amazon's vision?

"To be the world's most customer-centric company."

It sure is!

Hiring & Firing

The 6 Easy Steps To Hiring An A-Player

I was thrilled when I saw that Geoff Smart and Randy Street, of ghSMART, came out with the book Who: The A Method For Hiring on how to improve hiring. If you are involved in any hiring, I suggest you acquire this book right now!

You may recall that I had an incredible experience studying under Topgrading guru Brad Smart (Geoff's father) in Chicago a few years ago with Eben Pagan and some of the Hot Topic Media gang. It's good to see that the Smart family is even SMARTer than I thought!

"If you have anything to do with hiring, buy this book now!

I thought I would combine my learnings from reading *Who* with my those from reading the Topgrading book, taking the Topgrading seminar and conucting about 20 Topgrading/Who-inspired interviews since then.

The result is simple six steps to hiring an A-player (#s 3 and 5 were mentioned in my original Topgrading article -- Geoff and Randy add a lot in the other 4 steps and also simplify steps 3 and 5):

1) Create A Set Of Desired Outcomes

Craft a list out the outcomes you want the candidate to achieve in some initial time period.

Examples of outcomes include:

- Grow sales by 50% in year 1.

- Lead the launch of a major product launch by Q3.

- Hire 5 people by Q4.

Smart and Street call this list of outcomes a "Scorecard."

2) Hold A Screening Interview

The first interview with a candidate should include questions such as:

- What are your career goals?

- What are you really good at professionally?

- What are you not so great at or not interested in doing professionally?

- Topgrading is big on asking the candidate who their last 5 bosses were and how each will rate them on performance when you call them for a reference.

3) Hold An In-Depth Interview

For your in-depth interview with a candidate, it's wise to cover their entire career history as well as their experience in school.

Brad Smart calls this the Topgrading Interview (see A Mis-Hire Costs You 13X That Person's Salary: Why You Must Topgrade!)

You start with asking about College (if they attended) with simple ice-breaker questions like: how did you fit into school?; high/low points?; any awards/achievements?; greatest influence?; hold any jobs?; etc.

For the job-related questions, Brad's son Geoff and partner Randy Street have simplified the set of Topgrading questions to ask to things like:

- What were you hired to do?

- What accomplishments were you most proud of...and what were your low points?

- Who were the people you worked with and how would you rate them and they rate you

- Why did you leave that job?

4) The Focused Interviews

Smart and Street recommend that you then do a couple of more "focused" interviews in which you take one of your desired outcomes (E.g. Grow sales 50% in year 1) and then ask the candidate things like:

- What are some accomplishments you have in growing sales 50% or more?

- What are some mistakes and lessons you've learned in growing sales by 50%?

If another outcome you want is to lead the release of a major software product launch, then you ask the same questions about that.

5) Reference Interviews

As I mentioned in my Topgrading article, get in touch with at least a few of their references to go over the same types of questions you did with the applicant in the in-depth interview section (so you can cross-reference). So make sure to cover things like:

What were they hired to do?; What were ups and downs of their performance?; How would you rate their performance on a scale of 1 to 10? Then, describe the role you envision for the applicant and ask them what's a good fit and what's a bad fit.

6) Compare Your Interview Data With Desired Outcomes

The final step is to look at the data you've collected from the interviews & reference checks and compare it to the Scorecard and see how confident you feel that the candidate can achieve those outcomes.

Smart & Street recommend that if you feel 90% or more confident that the candidate has the skills and the desire to achieve the outcomes, then you have yourself an A-Player.

I've participated in about 20 interviews inspired by my learnings from Brad Smart, Geoff Smart and Randy Street; and my A-Player success rate has increased substantially.

"Money Ball": Finding Undervalued People

I was inspired by the book "Money Ball", by Michael Lewis, who chronicles the Oakland A's baseball team and its strategy of focusing on the undervalued players in the Major Leagues.

I read it well before the movie (with Brad Pitt) came out – and still haven't seen it!

I've found some success in applying this Moneyball approach to business. Specifically, I am always on the look out for undervalued people. Here are two examples of undervalued people I look for and find:

Fallen Stars

Fallen Stars are workers who hit a certain apex in their career and then for some reason fell, often far from that level. The reasons may include personal problems such as divorce, substance abuse or even criminal activity.

Such fallen stars are worth a close look to be given a second chance, especially if they proved themselves for a long period of time before their fall from grace.

I recall an attorney who was having a challenging time on the job market because one of his prior employers had run into trouble with the federal government and this had tainted the attorney's reputation. Closer scrutiny showed that he had done nothing wrong and in fact had a track record of 25 years of proven value! He was a fallen star.

Jack Welch, the former CEO of GE, points out that one of the best ways to earn trust and loyalty from someone is to help them out when they're down and out.

Diamonds in the Rough

A second example of undervalued people is what I refer to as "diamonds in the rough." Diamonds in the rough are different than fallen stars. As the label implies they are quite valuable individuals who are simply not appreciated for their potential. Diamonds in the rough usually exist because of poor managers or leaders surrounding the rough diamond.

A good place to look for such diamonds in the rough are mismanaged companies, as they sometimes forget to dig deep enough to find their diamonds.

A good sign of a mismanaged company is an ego driven management who typically takes their diamonds for granted. A great time to hire a diamond is when their employer is not doing so well in business, perhaps their sales have flattened or profits are down.

The diamond will have his or her antennae up a bit higher during those times and you can swoop in and hire them!

How To Give Feedback: The Simple 3-Step Sandwich Method

If you lead a person or team, have peers you work with or are managed by someone else (with no team that you're managing), the **Sandwich Method of Feedback** is an effective communication tool.

The Sandwich Method is so named because the pieces of bread represent positive feedback/compliments while the meat of the sandwich (or innards if you're vegetarian) represents constructive criticism.

I find this method of sandwiching the constructive criticism between two compliments to be an effective/disarming way to help improve/correct behaviour.

The Sandwich Method

1) Slice of Bread #1: Start off with positive feedback (authentic praise of something they did recently)

Examples:

"By the way, John, I have to hand it to you on that deal you closed yesterday...that goes a long way towards helping us reach our goal."

"Anne, I really appreciate you chipping in for Nicole this week while she was out of the office — that type of teamwork exemplifies the values I'm trying to instil at our company."

2) The "Meat of the Matter": Provide your constructive criticism

Be brief (yet clear and thorough) in your delivery of the meat of the matter — the criticism you want to share.

Ideally you are giving them constructive criticism on just one thing (at most two things)…I find criticism of three or more items is too much for a person to handle at one time. Additionally, try to give them the criticism in the context of how it can help them reach their goals.

Examples:

"Jon, you're so good at what you do that it's hard to ever find suggestions on how you can improve. That said, I know you really want that promotion to Director of Sales. One skill you're going to need in that position is analytics, and your weekly reports are currently pretty light on analytics. For you to earn that Director of Marketing spot, I recommend that you gain some mastery over analytics."

"Anne, I know this is tough for you to hear, but you are perceived by some on the team as cocky. And I know that you mentioned that you wanted a transfer to Customer Service — well, we certainly don't want them hearing that you have a reputation for cockiness. I recommend that you and I work together on making sure you're not perceived as cocky."

Caution About "Feelers": Be especially careful about giving criticism to sensitive people or "feelers" as many of us call them in Carl Jung personality type speak. If you're dealing with a sensitive/feeling type, I recommend you put in extra time on the Sandwich Method.

3) Slice Of Bread #2: End On A Positive Note

Ideas on how to end with positivity include:

*   You can simply reiterate the initial positive feedback/compliment you had given them.

- You can speak in general terms about how much progress they are making (read this article on How To Motivate Your Team Through Progress on page 146).

- You can compliment them on their receptiveness to receiving constructive criticism.

Examples:

"Jon, that deal you closed was really important and I'm thrilled with the fact that you and I can have an open conversation about working harder on analytics."

"Jon, I really admire your enthusiasm about developing yourself. You were already making headway and this analytics thing can be icing on the cake. I think it's a huge benefit in you progressing towards the Director of Sales position you covet."

"Anne, you're really on the right track here. This cockiness thing is just a bump in the road and I'm looking forward to working on it with you."

It should go without saying that all of your criticism (positive or negative) should be authentic and well thought out. That's the sandwich method…good luck with it!

How To Fire Someone (Includes A Script)

I've had to fire or let go a handful of people in my career. Firing someone can be tough, but if you follow these guidelines you should do just fine. Here is what I've learned:

Make The Decision Fast

The adage, "Fire Fast, Hire Slowly" is very true. On the firing side, I have never regretted firing someone who was a consistent problem. On the flip side, I have often regretted moving too slowly on firing someone. If your gut tells you that a person isn't working out, you owe it to your business and the employee in question to move fast.

Clarify The Reason You're Firing Them

You need to identify the reason that you're firing your employee (for yourself first; and then later to explain to the employee). It could be for performance or it could be that they did not fit into your culture. Whatever the case, have it well thought out for yourself and have specifics (examples or data) to back you up.

Document The Reason You're Firing Them

You should make sure that you or the hiring manager, document the reasons for the termination before the actual firing. The most common way to do this is in a performance review (also called a performance appraisal) in which you share your feedback with the employee in question.

I should write an entire article on performance reviews...but in the meantime, check out Performance Appraisal for more background.

The most important point is that the employee should not be surprised that they are not working out...and the details of this should be documented so that if the terminated employee ever tries to sue you for wrongful termination, you will have written details to show a judge.

Determine Their Last Day

Now that you've decided to be decisive (good for you!), you should determine when you'd like the person to leave. If the person you're firing has done something crooked, you may be choosing for their last day to be immediate.

In most cases, the person you're firing is just not performing to your standards or is not a good fit with your culture or values. In that case, I try to be consistent with all employees by using a standard amount of notice (2 weeks, 30 days, 2 months, etc.); though this may vary based on how long they've been with you or what their seniority is.

If you don't have a standard, then use your next firing to determine your standard (so that this is easier on you in the future!). If your company is small, like many I've worked in, it's ok for you to learn as you go!

Determine Their Final Deliverables

Figure out exactly what you need from them between the time you fire them and their last day. I prefer to make this list a fairly short list of deliverables to allow the fired employee to have some extra time to search for a job.

Determine Their Severance (if any)

Next you need to determine what severance payment if any you will pay them. Again, this should be consistent where possible. There should be a minimum severance package for an employee who had just recently joined the company (i.e. less than a year) and there can be extra severance based on longevity and seniority.

For example, some companies pay a minimum severance of 1 or 2 weeks to anyone they let go and then an additional week of severance for each additional period they've been there (e.g. an extra week of severance for every year they've been at the company)). Your industry may play by different rules so you should ask around.

And, again, if you don't have a standard set of severance packages yet, that's ok — you can use your next firing or two to establish one. The point is to be standard/consistent so that this will be easier for you in the future.

What to Say When Firing Someone (Write a Firing Script)

Now we're getting closer to having to actually fire the person. This is a very important conversation and I urge you to write out a script of what you're going to say.

Here's a script that I used to fire Cooper (don't worry, I've never fired a real Cooper before):

1. "Cooper, this isn't working out between us."

2. "The primary reason is [fill this in with the reason(s) that you already identified above] "E.g.: "Cooper, the reason this isn't working out is that we believe we need a more experienced person in your position to help us reach our objectives."

3. "We value you immensely, Coop (list all his contributions and really make him feel loved)."

4. "And what we'd like to do is give you time to figure out your transition." (This is optional based on when you determined their last day to be).

5. "Since we know it's easier to find a job while still an employee, you can remain a paid employee until (fill in the date) "

6. "Between now and (fill in the date), we ask that you complete the following deliverables, and you can feel free to use your remaining time as "flex time" to search for a job.

7. "We'll do our best in supporting whatever next job you get." (e.g. You say you'll be willing to act as a reference, assuming you see some positive things in the person, or at least will confirm that they worked at your company).

Dress Rehearsal

I recommend you practice the script with a fellow executive, your manager or a mentor. Do a dry run-through together — it will make you much more comfortable with the difficult conversation you're about to have. Really dig into what Cooper's pain point is going to be regarding his imminent employment termination. It may be that he's driven by extra money (i.e. severance) or it may be that it's very important for him to save face.

The Actual Firing

Ok, now comes the part you probably fear the most (I did too): You have to tell the employee that he or she is out of here.

Here's what I do:

- **Follow the Script** — I go through the script (see previous page) step by step from memory (I keep the bullets in front of me on a notepad just in case)

- **Listen** — After going through the script, I sit back and do nothing but listen. It is very likely that Cooper is now going to begin experiencing the "5 Stages of Loss" (especially the first three or four):

  o **Denial** — Cooper may deny the reasons that you give him for termination.

- ○ **Anger** — Cooper may become angry either at you or someone else in your organization who he tries to blame.

- ○ **Bargaining/Negotiation** — Cooper may begin to negotiate (i.e. offering to take another position or lower pay, etc.).

- ○ **Depression** — Cooper will likely experience this most after the meeting is over.

- ○ **Acceptance** — Cooper will eventually accept the decision.

- **Stay Firm** — Cooper may argue that it's an unfair termination — stick with your script and decision. Don't send mixed signals.

- **Be Compassionate** — This is going to be hard for Cooper, so show compassion.

- **Be Respectful** — Treat Cooper with the utmost respect, regardless of the circumstances — Take the high road!

Most of the time, Cooper will eventually accept the decision; though he may try to bargain a bit in which case you should be open to exceptions to any of the terms you outlined if Cooper makes a strong case). But if you've done your homework, your severance and timing will have been fair and Cooper will accept it.

Other Things To Consider

- **Getting Cooper to Sign a Release** — Get the person you've fired to agree that they accept the severance terms along with their final deliverables and what their last day of employment (this can be in print or email).

- **Termination Letter (aka Notice of Termination)** — Cooper may ask you for a termination letter…you should give it to him with the basics mentioned in the 7 Steps on the previous pages (keep it short and to the point).

- **Communicating that the Employee is Leaving** — If Cooper is managing people, you may consider allowing Cooper to communicate his departure to his team (to save face); otherwise, it will be Cooper's manager's responsibility to communicate Cooper's departure to team members (keep the message simple and tell others they can contact you directly if you have specific questions).

- **The Threat of a Wrongful Termination (or Unlawful Termination) Suit** — If you have followed all the steps and have documentation of the situation, it is rare that Cooper will sue you. If he does, you will be prepared with documentation to get a fair hearing.

A final reminder that I can't emphasize enough: Deal with the issue swiftly. You owe it to your company, yourself and Cooper to be decisive. Plus, the sooner you act the more flexibility you have in helping Cooper on his way (and the more money and headaches you save everyone). And if you want to minimize the number of people you fire, please read You Must Topgrade.

Thank You!

Each of the 9 cool illustrations inside An Enlightened Entrepreneur were created by the Los Angeles artist Miles Lasalle (who also happens to be my nephew!). Miles can be reached at mileslasalle@gmail.com.

The back cover photo of me was taken by Wendy K. Yalom, an award winning wedding and portrait photographer in San Francisco, California (she's also my yoga teacher!). Wendy can be reached at Studio@wendykyalom.com or found on the web at www.wendykyalom.com.

'n the USA
'n. SC
04 No\. 2012